# AN ARK FOR THE POOR

## THE STORY OF L'ARCHE

## Other books by Jean Vanier

**with Darton, Longman and Todd, London**
*Tears of Silence* (1970)
*Man and Woman He Made Them* (1988)
*Community and Growth* (1989)
*The Broken Body* (1989)
*Treasures of the Heart* (1989)

**with Paulist Press, Mahwah, New Jersey**
*Eruption to Hope* (1971)
*Be Not Afraid* (1975)
*I Meet Jesus* (1986)
*I Walk With Jesus* (1987)
*Man and Woman He Made Them* (1988)
*Community and Growth* (1989)
*The Broken Body* (1989)
*From Brokenness to Community* (1992)

**with The Crossroad Press, New York**
*Jesus, the Gift of Love* (1994)

**with Gill & Macmillan Ltd., Dublin**
*Be Not Afraid* (1975)
*Followers of Jesus* (1975, 1993)

**with Griffin House, Toronto**
*Tears of Silence* (1970)
*Eruption to Hope* (1971)
*In Weakness, Strength* (1975)

**with Hodder & Stoughton**
*Jesus, the Gift of Love* (1994)
*The Door of Hope* (1995)

**with Lancelot Press, Hantsport, Nova Scotia**
*Images of Love, Words of Hope* (1991)
*Network of Friends* (2 volumes) (1992, 1994)

**with Meakin, Ottawa**
*Treasures of the Heart* (1989)

# AN ARK FOR THE POOR

## THE STORY OF L'ARCHE

**Jean Vanier**

NOVALIS / GEOFFREY CHAPMAN / CROSSROAD

Photos: L'Arche

© 1995 Novalis

Novalis
49 Front Street, East, 2nd Floor,
Toronto, Ontario, Canada, M5E 1B3

The Crossroad Publishing Company
370 Lexington Avenue, New York, NY 10017

Geoffrey Chapman (a Cassell imprint)
Wellington House, 125 Strand, London WC2R 0BB

Scripture quotations are taken from the New Revised Standard Version of
the Bible, © 1989, Division of Christian Education of the National Council
of Churches of Christ in the United States, and are used with permission.

Canadian Cataloguing in Publication Data
Vanier, Jean, 1928-
An ark for the poor: the story of L'Arche
(L'Arche collection)
Issued also in French under title: L'histoire de L'Arche.
ISBN 2-89088-731-6
1. Arche (Association)--History. 2. Church work with the mentally handi-
capped. 3. Caring--Religious aspects--Christianity. 4. Vanier, Jean, 1928-
I. Title. II. Series
HV3008.F72V36   1995    267.182        C95-900379-7

British Library Cataloguing-in-Publication Data
A catalogue record for this book is available from the British Library
ISBN 0-225-66804-1

Library of Congress Catalog Card No.: 95-69126
ISBN 0-8245-1538-2

Printed and bound in Canada

*Father Thomas Philippe, o.p., died on February 4, 1993.*
*At L'Arche we grieved his death.*
*He was at the heart of L'Arche.*
*He encouraged me,*
*and inspired me to begin the community.*
*He walked with us all*
*and he nourished us spiritually.*
*He continues to walk with us*
*in the heart of God.*
*This book is dedicated to him.*

# CONTENTS

# INTRODUCTION

L'Arche is thirty years old! Yet we are probably just at the beginning of our history.

When I came to live with Raphaël Simi and Philippe Seux in Trosly-Breuil, France, in August 1964, I knew that it was an irreversible act, but I had no idea what the future would be. I never imagined that L'Arche would grow in many countries and embrace diverse cultures. As I write this history, I am full of gratitude as I see how God has been guiding us over these thirty years. God has used everything, even our poverty, our limits and our errors, as well as our gifts, so that L'Arche could become God's work. Hence the story of L'Arche is truly a sacred history.

God wanted L'Arche to be a new form of family: a family of the poor that rises above prejudice and fear of difference, a family witnessing that the only way to build peace and unity is to recognize our own poverty and our need for others. Our littleness and our weakness keep us united in L'Arche. Like every other family's history, ours is a mixture of successes and failures. It is the story of people who continue to live in L'Arche or who have been part of the family for a short time. It is the story, especially, of the beauty and fragility of people with mental handicaps. In and through the simple, humble gestures of daily living, it continues to be written, day after day. Our people help us rediscover the importance of these little gestures.

As I write our history, I try to recall the past. I realize that I cannot tell the whole story. There would be so many beautiful stories to tell, so many events in each of our communities that touch our people's lives—stories of pain and suffering, but also of little miracles. This is not just the history of individual people, but of L'Arche as an organization, a family. Since I write it from my own limited experience, it is necessarily incomplete. For example, I do not describe the whole development of L'Arche in other European countries or in North America. This account is based mainly on my own experience in my community, which is rooted in a Roman Catholic context, as well as my experience with L'Arche's international structures.

Being in L'Arche does not mean following an ideal or practising a certain philosophy. Being in L'Arche means being part of a history that already exists; it means belonging to a people. Throughout our history we have tried to discern the signs of God and the Spirit's ways for L'Arche. Just as the Jewish people have kept a sense of tradition, we too recognize the importance of re-reading our history to remember the essential, which can at times be obscured. In L'Arche we love to celebrate our history because it lets us give thanks for all we have received. Living in L'Arche with people who have mental handicaps has made me realize how important it is to help them rediscover their own personal histories. Because they have often been rejected and seen as different, they tend to feel as though they do not belong to human history. Since they have been deprived of intellectual means and are not integrated into the usual networks that others around them take for granted—school, college or university studies, job, marriage, parenting—they have few reference points for their own personal histories. It is as if they had no past. We have discovered how important it is to celebrate birthdays in L'Arche, to help these persons recognize and re-read their personal histories and, if possible, be in contact with their own families. Birthday celebrations provide a chance to emphasize certain stages in their lives, highlight their gifts, laugh about their faults or failures, and celebrate each one's unique gifts. In the same way, what I have said about each person can also be said for each community.

I did not realize the full meaning of L'Arche when, inspired by Fr. Thomas, I started living with Raphaël and Philippe. I discovered what L'Arche was called to be as I lived each day, trying to be faithful to the needs of those who had come to create community with me. We still discover L'Arche's meaning each day, in each community and each new culture. When I began, I was far from imagining the various facets of community life and all the power contained in the message of life with the poor. Today in 1995, I am still discovering what L'Arche is. It is important to keep this openness to what is given to us each day. So many movements and communities were inspired in the beginning, but ended up as institutions when they lost their sense of history and their openness to new inspirations and orientations. We are a people on a journey, walking in insecurity but certain that God is watching over us. It is up to us to be attentive to God and open to the future, and to accept challenges humbly so that our lives remain centred on what is essential to our community life.

## A question of language

Language has evolved a great deal over the last thirty years. People used to talk about the "mentally retarded" or the "mentally deficient." Today we use other terms: "people with learning disabilities" or "people who are mentally challenged." Language evolves according to cultures, countries and times. Behind the changes in language is the desire to affirm that a person with a mental handicap is first and foremost a person who should be respected and given the opportunity to exercise his or her particular gifts.

In this book, I have kept the phrase "people with mental handicaps." They are truly *people* with all the implications that this word holds. Each person is unique and important. Yet there is difference. Some people come or are sent to L'Arche because of their handicaps; others choose freely to come and live with them. The important thing in language is to signify difference while respecting persons.

Sometimes today people have difficulty with the phrases "the poor" and " the weak." The gospel message talks about the "poor," which is frequently interpreted as the "economically poor." But a person without work and a parent who has lost a child are also poor. The poor person is one in need who recognizes the need and cries out for help. Weakness is frequently considered a defect. However, little children are weak; they cannot fend for themselves. People with severe mental handicaps are weak; they cannot cope all alone. This does not mean that they have no value. They need someone who can walk with them. In this book I have occasionally used the words "poor" and "weak," and I am aware that they go against certain cultural norms that want everyone to be strong and powerful. We all have our limits and handicaps. We all need each other. But some people recognize their poverty; others do not.

**Special thanks**

I would like to thank in a special way Katryn Harris who took time during her holidays to go through and retype the whole English text of this book.

*Jean Vanier*
*January 1995*

I

# The founding of L'Arche
## (1964-1969)

### The call

At the invitation of Dr. Robert Préaut, Father Thomas Philippe, o.p., came to Trosly in the autumn of 1963, to be the chaplain of the Val Fleuri, a small institution for men with mental handicaps. The Val had been founded by Mr. André Prat for his son, Jean-Pierre.

I went to visit Fr. Thomas around Christmas, 1963. I was deeply impressed by the men who had become Fr. Thomas's friends. He had sensed their spiritual openness and their place in God's heart. Each one had so much life, had suffered so profoundly and thirsted so deeply for friendship. Within each gesture and each word was the question: "Will you come back?" "Do you love me?" Their cry of pain and their thirst for love touched me deeply.

Fr. Thomas, in his gentle way, suggested that maybe I could begin "something." It was, in fact, a very opportune moment. There was a great need for homes and workshops for people with mental handicaps; the French government was ready to give the necessary financial support.

In January 1964, I went to Toronto, Canada, to teach moral philosophy at St. Michael's College. I loved teaching but, at the same time, I did not feel that Jesus wanted me to stay there. When I returned to France, I went back to see Fr.

Thomas: the same gentle hint, the same question. Without having any big vision (that's not my way) it seemed quite clear that Jesus wanted me to do something. I was—and am still—quite naive. I didn't ask too many questions. I was open and available; I wanted to follow Jesus and live the way of the gospel. So, encouraged by Fr. Thomas and Dr. Préaut, a psychiatrist who was chairman of the Board of Directors responsible for the Val Fleuri, I decided to do "something." I went to see the person in charge of institutions for people with handicaps in the local area. He confirmed me in my decision.

At the beginning of it all God's call was revealed to me through Fr. Thomas. L'Arche was not my project, but God's.

## The need

I began to visit different centres for people with mental handicaps. I was quite overwhelmed by what I saw, especially in an asylum south of Paris. Huge concrete walls surrounded the buildings made of cement block; eighty men lived in dormitories with no work. All day long they just walked around in circles. From 2 to 4 p.m. there was a compulsory siesta, then time for a walk all together. There I was struck by the screams and the atmosphere of sadness, but also by a mysterious presence of God. In that asylum I met Philippe Seux and Raphaël Simi for the first time. Both had been placed there following the death of their parents.

With the help of my parents and friends, I was able to buy a small house in Trosly-Breuil. The walls were quite solid but the inside needed many repairs. In July 1964, I met Dan Berrigan, a Jesuit I had known in New York a few years earlier. We ate together in a small restaurant near Place St. Sulpice in Paris. I told him about my plans. He spoke to me about Louis Pretty, a Canadian architect who wanted to give one or two years of his life to a project in the service of the poor. A few weeks later I met Louis, who agreed to come and help. It was important to have a few people to be able to

*L'Arche's first house at Trosly-Breuil*

begin. We did not have much money. We rented a small truck and went to buy some second-hand furniture from Abbé Pierre's Emmaus community. Dr. Préaut also lent and gave us some furniture.

We had to create a legal structure that would be responsible for what was about to come into being. Dr. Préaut suggested that we become part of an already established charitable society that would then take care of L'Arche's administrative aspects. I accepted on two conditions: that I become the chairman and appoint half of the members of the Board.

In June—even before we had the house—I had decided to open the community on August 4 or 5: either August 4 because it was St. Dominic's feast day (and Fr. Thomas was a Dominican) or August 5 because it was a special feast of Mary. On August 4, the director of the asylum in the Seine-et-Marne brought Raphaël, Philippe and Dany to the house, along with a meal for everyone. (Dany was a deeply emotionally disturbed man who could not hear or speak. He was

17

living so much in his own world of pain and dreams that he could not stay with us for more than one day.) After a festive meal that Dr. and Mrs. Préaut and Father Thomas shared with us, I was left alone with Raphaël, Philippe and Dany. We were all a bit lost. Jean-Louis Coic, a long-time friend, was there to help out a bit. Louis Pretty was to come in September or October.

And that is how L'Arche began. I knew that my welcoming Raphaël and Philippe was a point of no return. I was conscious of a covenant between us. All I wanted was to create a community of which they would be the centre and give them a family, a place of belonging where all aspects of their beings could grow and discover the good news of Jesus.

*Jean Vanier and Philippe Seux*

## Simplicity and poverty

Simplicity and poverty characterized L'Arche's beginnings. The house was poor and had no toilets (we had set up a pail in the garden!). There was one tap and one wood-burning stove. Jean-Louis or I would take turns preparing the meals. Raphaël and Philippe helped as well as they could with the different tasks in the house and the garden. We began to get to know each other and do things together. We were learning how to live together, care for one another, listen to one another, have fun and pray together. I thought I had the right to tell Raphaël and Philippe what to do. For me it was normal that everyone get up and go to 7 o'clock Mass every day! I didn't ask their opinion about that or anything else. It took time for me to understand that I had to listen more and that they had their own lives, their own expectations and their own desires. My way of doing things was still that of a naval officer!

This poverty attracted many friends: Madame Bertrand, an elderly woman in the village, brought us soup every Friday; Monsieur Roland did some carpentry work for us. We received food packages in the mail. Madame Lepère, Mademoiselle Gsell and Madame Morinvillé gave us vegetables and apples. Mlle Edé helped us and Antoinette Maurice came and did the cooking every Monday. Many friends from the area came because they knew Fr. Thomas, who was living in great poverty in the sacristy behind his little chapel. They would come together one evening a week for a gospel sharing which I gave, followed by a time of silent prayer and adoration. Little by little, a small Christian community was being built around L'Arche and Fr. Thomas: Raphaël and Philippe benefited a great deal from these new friends. They were happy to have left their institution.

Father Thomas and I had other friends, such as Jacqueline d'Halluin and Gerry MacDonald, who came to Trosly a few days each week to help out. When there are few assistants, it is good to have friends who come regularly to help with the various tasks in the community.

On August 22, Henri Wambergue came to live with us. I knew his sister, Sister Marie-Madeleine, a Carmelite nun in Abbeville. For many months, she, with her Carmelite community, had been carrying this project in their hearts and prayers. She has been praying for L'Arche for over thirty years now.

During those first months, I learned a great deal. I was beginning to discover the immense amount of pain hidden in the hearts of Raphaël, Philippe and so many of their brothers and sisters. I sensed how much their hearts had been broken by rejection, abandonment and lack of respect. At the same time, I was beginning to discover some of the beauty and gentleness of their hearts, their capacity for communion and tenderness. I was beginning to sense how living with them could transform me, not through awakening and developing my qualities of leadership and intelligence, but by awakening the qualities of my heart, the child within me.

**With Father Thomas**

Fr. Thomas and I shared the deep conviction that Jesus had called us together to accomplish something. This fundamental unity between us was never shaken: it was L'Arche's foundation. Fr. Thomas had a meal with us from time to time, but he did not get involved in daily tasks. He wanted to keep a certain freedom in order to live his priesthood fully and to pray for us—L'Arche, the people in the village and surrounding area. As he was a man of prayer, many came to see him to ask for guidance.

**The name and prayer of L'Arche**

Shortly after the opening of the house, I asked Jacqueline d'Halluin to look in the bible for names for the house. She suggested about a hundred names. When she said "L'Arche," I knew without any hesitation that was it. She knew it, too.

But it was only later on that I realized all the symbolism behind this biblical name. Noah's ark, built on God's command, is the boat of salvation. The passages in Genesis (6:1-9:17) which tell the story of Noah are rich and meaningful. The ark reminds us of the first covenant between God and humanity, even before the birth of the Jewish people. And the Fathers of the Church referred to Mary, who carried within her womb the Saviour, as "the Ark of the Covenant." It is a beautiful name.

Jacqueline also wrote the L'Arche prayer following a few notes I had given her. The three invocations "Lord, bless us through the eyes of your poor ones; Lord, smile on us through the eyes of your poor ones; Lord, receive us one day in the company of your poor ones" come from St. Vincent de Paul. In 1974, Jean de la Selle and François Vidil, a Little Brother of Jesus put that prayer to music. In 1970, Gabrielle Einsle and I wrote a L'Arche prayer respecting the inter-faith nature of Asha Niketan for our community in India. In 1973, Thérèse Vanier and Ann and Geoffrey Morgan at Little Ewell wrote a prayer in English inspired by the initial L'Arche prayer and by the new community's ecumenical vocation.

## The *Letters of L'Arche*

From the very beginning of L'Arche I realized the importance of sharing what we were living and learning through "Letters to Friends." In my first letter, dated August 22, 1964, I wrote:

> With the increasing number of friends of L'Arche, I find I have to write to you by means of a circular letter. I'm sure you won't hold it against me. Most of all I want to keep you up to date with how our work is developing. I will send you a circular letter from time to time, with a few articles on different subjects which touch our work. I hope they will become visible signs which unite us all.

Then I gave some news: "There is still a lot to do in the house. But the garden has already been cleared and vegetables planted. We are awaiting the arrival of two ducks, two chickens and one rabbit!"

Although the letters have developed quite a lot since then, their function remains the same: to provide a link of communion and a place to tell others what we are living and discovering in L'Arche.

In January, 1971, we began printing *Letters of L'Arche.*

## Open to Providence and daily life

When I began L'Arche, I had no preconceived ideas. I did not know much about the world of people with mental handicaps. I lived from day to day, trying to adapt to circumstances and events. I did plan to build a few sheds on the land next to the house; I had even bought a prefabricated wood building from a demolition contractor. It was never put up.

In September, Dr. Préaut asked us to welcome Jacques Dudouit. Then, in November, Sr. Marie Benoît arrived. She was living in the village with two other sisters and asked to come and work in the community. So we began to eat better! On December 8, a social worker asked us to welcome Jean-Pierre Crépieux. Little by little the family was growing. But I had no idea where we were going. I was happy but quite naive in this new life together. I put my trust in Jesus and had the sense that he was watching over us.

Our first house, L'Arche, in its poverty and the welcome it offered to Raphaël, Philippe, Jacques, Jean-Pierre and others, had a prophetic element to it. We prayed together; we wanted to learn to love each other and create a warm, open and welcoming home. We had no big worries; the neighbours loved and supported us.

In my mind and heart, I did have models of community life that I was following more or less consciously. I was influenced by my contacts with one community in Canada and two in the United States that in many ways resembled each another: Montreal's Bénédict Labre House, founded by Tony Walsh, and New York's The Catholic Worker, founded by Dorothy Day, and Friendship House, founded by Catherine Doherty. In these three communities lay people lived poorly with poor street people. I had also been influenced by Montreal's Foyer de Charité, founded by Cardinal Léger after his visit to Turin's Foyer of Cottalengo. This community lived in a spirit of prayer and welcomed people with severe mental handicaps.

### The Val Fleuri: a turning point

At the end of December 1964, Dr. Préaut and Mr. Prat informed me that all the staff at the Val Fleuri had resigned. They asked me to take on the directorship starting March 22, 1965. I was astounded. The Val was big: it housed thirty-two men. My contact with the Val during those first months of L'Arche had been very limited. We used to go there to shower while the men of the Val were at work. Apart from that, there was little contact. I felt the staff distrusted me a little because I was Dr. Préaut's friend. I found the Val noisy and closed in on itself. Every day the thirty-two men would go out all together for a walk along the roads of Trosly. Joseph and Charles, the two instructors in charge of the house, would be with them, one in front of, the other behind the group. Other than that, the men at the Val did not have permission to go out to the village. As individuals these men were kind and good, and I was drawn to them, but together they formed quite an explosive group. However, I still said yes to Dr. Préaut's request. I felt I could not do otherwise. Fr. Thomas encouraged me, too; it seemed to follow the pattern of things, and be what Jesus wanted.

I well remember that day, March 22, 1965, when I took charge of the Val Fleuri. It was a Sunday morning. Monsieur Wattier, the former director, gave me the keys, showed me

23

the account books and then said "Au revoir." Joseph and Charles agreed to stay on for a few months but all the rest of the staff from the workshops, the garden and the infirmary left. I found myself director of a small institution. I felt terribly alone. Madame Lepère, a friend from Cuise-La-Motte, a nearby village, agreed to take on the housekeeping.

Gerry MacDonald took on the work program. Anne-Marie Morinvillé from Trosly came to work in the workshop. A few months later her sister Annie came. At first there was no nurse. Every morning I had to give Denis an injection since he had diabetes. If you could have seen me practising on an orange! Then Yvonne Collet, a nurse from Compiègne, started to come regularly for a few hours each day.

My first act as director of the Val was to lose the bunch of keys! I think one of the men hid them to show his anger at my arrival. When I think about all that today, I don't know how I coped. It was crazy. There were few assistants and the men at the Val were so difficult and explosive. Luckily I was a bit naive. I sensed that Jesus was present in and through all the difficulties and even the chaos, and that he would help us. Only by the grace of God could I keep going because, humanly speaking, it was impossible.

Some women from the village came to do the cooking and the housework: Madame Welikij, Madame Journeau, Madame Cagniard, Madame Didelet and Mademoiselle Jean. Their presence and their warm affection for the men were vital supports. I used to have my noon meal at the Val and my evening meal at L'Arche (that was my relaxation!). My office and bedroom were at the Val. I must admit I didn't sleep much during those first few years: there was so much noise during the night!

When we assumed responsibility for the Val, another aspect of L'Arche emerged. We needed to meet state standards and establish links with local government officials and the Ministry of Labour; we needed to cooperate with professionals. I had to learn about government grants and salaries. L'Arche was no longer a small, prophetic community where we were living poorly with the poor. There was a budget to draw up and an accounts sheet to balance. This change, however, did not alter L'Arche's prophetic and evangelical nature, which remains its foundation. It was as such that I presented L'Arche when I met the then newly-appointed Bishop of Beauvais, Bishop Desmazières. God wanted L'Arche to begin this way so that it could be a place where assistants could live a radical commitment with the poor, in the name of Jesus, for the kingdom. But with the Val, God had added another dimension. He showed us that L'Arche should not only be a prophetic and marginalised community, but also one rooted in the structures of the state.

Another important event at that time was my meeting with Dr. Léone Richet at a conference for professionals in Paris. I gave a talk on the importance of community life for people with mental handicaps. Dr. Richet must have found what I said a bit naive, even crazy. After my talk, she came up to talk to me and we became friends. At that time she was a psychiatrist working in the children's department of the Psychiatric Hospital of Clermont, forty kilometers from Trosly. She played a vital role during those first years, helping us to better understand the psychological pain and needs of the men at the Val, some of whom were quite disturbed, and how we could help them. She was the first person to help us grasp L'Arche's specific therapy. She came regularly a few hours a week for several years. When she left the region, she managed to find another psychiatrist who would continue to help and support us, Dr. Erol Franko. He had the same qualities as Dr. Richet, and also became our friend. He played a vital role in my intellectual formation and in the development of L'Arche's therapeutic approach.

And that is how—just a few months after its foundation—L'Arche had become a body of more than fifty people with links to the state, professionals, the Board of Directors and the church. I was both director of a small institution and shepherd of a small Christian community centred on the poor, where many did not express their faith. How could we maintain unity in all this? That was the challenge.

## The vocation of people with handicaps

Throughout all these questions and difficulties (and they were many!), I began to see more clearly the role of people with handicaps, and thus the specific vocation of L'Arche. Visitors were struck, as I myself had been, by these men who, although they were so poor and rejected, were such bearers of life and love. They are so different from intellectuals or people who have power, who often live behind masks or think they are superior and hide their hearts. People with mental handicaps are so spontaneous and true! Their thirst for friendship, love and communion leaves no one indifferent: either you harden your heart to their cry and reject them, or you open your heart and enter into a relationship built on trust, simple, tender gestures and few words. Hidden in those who are powerless is a mysterious power: they attract and awaken the heart. In the little house of L'Arche, we had times of celebration, feast days and birthdays; we laughed a lot together. We were happy to be together (that doesn't mean that there were not also difficult times, crises and violence). We were beginning to discover that people with mental handicaps are not first of all "problems" or sources of death; if we welcome them just as they are, if we communicate with them and enter into communion with them, then they can become truly a source of life that awakens our hearts and calls us to community life.

## L'Arche in heaven

In the autumn of 1964, Marguerite Bilodeau, a Canadian friend, came to Paris to work as a secretary for the National Film Board of Canada. When she left Canada, she sent all her furniture to L'Arche. She would often spend her weekends and holidays in Trosly. I can still hear her crystal clear laughter!

Marguerite died in May 1965, the same day that Mira Ziauddin arrived in Trosly. Marguerite was buried in Trosly. She loved L'Arche and had offered her life to God for the community.

Since then someone from almost every community has returned to the Father.

One of the most moving deaths was in Asha Niketan, Bangalore, in 1971. Kanna, a young man with a handicap, fell into a well. The community found him a few hours later. His father came, accompanied by a Hindu priest who said, "When a work is of God, a just man dies." Words of truth, words of compassion, words from God. Over these thirty years, many just men and women have died as an offering and a gift to the Father for L'Arche.

## II

# EXPANSION BEGINS

## (1969-1972)

### The seeds of expansion

In a short document written just a few months after the foundation of L'Arche, I spoke about welcoming people who had other difficulties—old people and people with physical handicaps—in the property that was for sale next door to L'Arche. From the very beginning, I had not thought of limiting our welcome to Raphaël and Philippe. I was more a man of action than someone ready to live quietly with a few people. However, I had no idea of starting a movement or establishing communities outside of Trosly, and even less outside of France! At one moment I had even said that we should stay the size of one car load—and not grow any bigger—so that if no one came to help me I could at least continue to travel by bringing everyone in the car.

Something that happened between Christmas 1964 and March 1965 helped me clarify the objectives of the new community. On Christmas day, as I coming back from the train station in Compiègne, I saw a man walking along the road. I stopped to give him a lift. He was a man named Gabriel who lived on the streets. I invited him to stay with us for Christmas. The night before he left, I invited him to come back—which he did, in February. He spent a few weeks with us, working with Philippe, Raphaël, Jacques, Jean-Pierre and

Henri. But he seemed to find it difficult to be with them. One day his anger exploded, and he started to throw plates around, traumatizing Raphaël and the others. It was clear that L'Arche was not right for him; we had to send him away. That was not an easy thing for me to do, but from it I learned how important it is to be clear in our priorities. We had to know whom L'Arche was for. I was already committed to Raphaël, Philippe and the others; I did not have the right to welcome someone who would endanger their lives. When I took on the directorship of the Val Fleuri in March 1965, it became even clearer that L'Arche was destined for people with mental handicaps.

Perhaps I never was a very good assistant, and even less a good model, but God seems to have made use of my capacity for action, work and leadership as well as my desire to live the gospel and serve the poor to begin L'Arche, help it grow and guide its first steps. My lectures in Toronto, Faith and Sharing Retreats in Canada and the Faith and Light pilgrimage to Lourdes in 1971 (the preparations began in 1968) prepared the way for L'Arche's expansion.

*Lectures in Canada*

After a lecture series I gave in 1964 at St. Michael's College (affiliated with the University of Toronto), I was invited back each year to give courses in philosophy. The subjects of these courses varied: friendship and affectivity, artistic inspiration, the cry of the poor. They seemed to attract many students in search of faith witnesses. Other universities also invited me. It was the post-Vatican II era when there was much confusion in the church and among students. During one of these courses I met Robert Larouche, who was to become involved with L'Arche. Then, in 1965, I was invited, along with William Stringfellow, to a large ecumenical meeting in Montreal for theology students from different churches. Bill Clarke S.J. and Steve Newroth both attended that meeting. Both came to Trosly afterwards.

## Faith and Sharing retreats

Following the lectures which, through God's grace, attracted many students, I was asked to give a retreat to the priests in the diocese of Toronto. This invitation took me by surprise. I felt incapable of giving any immediate answer. I needed time to pray and reflect. Finally, it seemed quite clear that Jesus wanted me to answer "yes," but with three conditions: that it be a silent retreat, that it last eight days, and that it be open, not only to priests, but also to religious and lay people. The retreat took place in August 1968, at Marylake near Toronto. I was naive (as always) and petrified, yet at the same time I trusted in Jesus. I had entrusted this retreat to the prayers of the French Carmelites in Abbeville and in Cognac (where I had prepared my talks). I must admit, however, that when I walked into that office marked "Retreat Master," I didn't feel very sure of myself.

The retreat was grace-filled: the talks, the eucharist, our times of silence, the sharing in groups of eight where each of us could share (but not discuss!) our faith. The times of adoration seemed to touch people. I had learned the importance of adoration with the Little Sisters of Jesus in Montreal. At the end of the retreat there was such a deep unity between us that nobody wanted to leave. That is why a group of retreatants decided to prepare two other retreats the following year, one organized by Sue Mosteller for former retreatants, and one that I would give at Marylake.

About sixty people attended the Marylake retreat, among them Sue Mosteller, Gabrielle Einsle, Colleen Walsh, Marie Paradis and John Dare. Each of them became involved in L'Arche later on. Sr. Rosemarie Donovan, the superior of Our Lady's Missionaries, was also there. At the end of the retreat, she offered L'Arche their former novitiate house in

Richmond Hill, just north of Toronto. This is the house where, in 1969, Steve and Ann Newroth began Daybreak on their return from Europe. That is how L'Arche was born in Canada. From that first retreat, Faith and Sharing, a movement to organize retreats of the same kind, was born in Canada and the United States. I would be invited to different cities and, after the retreats, groups would be appointed to prepare similar retreats the following year. New L'Arche communities were often born after such retreats. George and Doris Myers started a community in Edmonton, and Pat and Jo Lenon in Calgary, Alberta; Margaret O'Donnell in Victoria, British Columbia; Marie Paradis in Winnipeg, Manitoba; Paul Rancourt in St. Malachie, Québec; Jan Risse in Mobile, Alabama; Pat Wehner in Cleveland, Ohio; Fr. George Strohmeyer and Sr. Barbara Karznia in Erie, Pennsylvania.

As I re-read our history I realize how important these retreats have been, both for me personally and for L'Arche. They helped me discover the power of the word of God that is the good news announced to the poor, a promise of Jesus' presence and his forgiveness. This word purifies, liberates and reveals to each of us our true identity as a beloved son or beloved daughter of the Father, and awakens in us new energies of love. As I proclaim the word, I often feel that I am the first one who needs to hear it! It does me a lot of good, even though I realize that I am far from living what I proclaim.

These retreats have been important for L'Arche, for they have not only enabled us to expand, but have also reminded us that, before being a good home for people with handicaps, L'Arche is founded on the gospel. For people with handicaps, even more important than "normalization" is their growth in love, openness, service and holiness, which is the ultimate purpose of each human person. This growth in love does not exclude in any way doing all we can to help each person acquire knowledge and independence or be well integrated into the life of society and of the church. In fact, it emphasizes their importance.

## Faith and Light

Faith and Light is like a first cousin to L'Arche. It was founded after a meeting with Marie-Hélène Mathieu, General Secretary at the *Office chrétien pour les personnes avec un handicap* (Christian office for people with mental handicaps) in Paris. Marie-Hélène herself had been deeply touched by her meeting with Gérard and Camille Proffit who wanted to organize a pilgrimage to Lourdes in which their two sons, both with severe mental handicaps, could participate. At L'Arche we had discovered the importance of making pilgrimages together. Walking together and travelling together to a holy place, a place of prayer, is very important for everyone, but even more so for people with mental handicaps and for the poor. Throughout the centuries, Jewish, Moslem and Hindu people, as well as Christians, have always had a deep sense of pilgrimage. With Marie-Hélène, we decided to organize an international pilgrimage with people who have mental handicaps and their parents and friends, especially young people. It took place at Easter 1971 at Lourdes and was an important time of celebration and joy. Twelve thousand people from fourteen countries participated. Many parents discovered that they were not alone, that their son or daughter was not a source of shame, and that they could celebrate together. For many young people it was a time of presence and commitment to people with mental handicaps; for those with mental handicaps, it was a moment of joy and a meeting with God.

After that pilgrimage we discovered that the Holy Spirit wanted more than a pilgrimage. It was the beginning of a new community movement. Faith and Light communities have now been born throughout the world. These communities bring together people with mental handicaps, their parents and friends, and meet regularly to celebrate together and support each other. They want to be communities that are signs of the kingdom, where the poor truly find their place. In 1995, there are more than 1,200 communities in seventy countries.

Through Faith and Light, people have discovered their vocation to share their life with people who have handicaps; they have decided to join L'Arche or to found new L'Arche communities. Through Faith and Light the following communities were started: le Toit in Belgium by Fr. André Roberti; Nil Steensens Hus in Denmark by Fr. Jorgen Hviid; la Rose des Vents in France by Camille Proffit; Little Ewell in England by my sister, Thérèse; Il Chicco in Rome by Gwenda Malwezza; la Rocha in Brazil by Maria Silvia and la Corolle in Switzerland by Pierre Epiney.

## Expansion in and around Trosly

After the Val became our responsibility, L'Arche grew rapidly. In many ways I felt completely out of my depth before the number and the situations of the men who lived there. Some needed to leave the larger group of the Val for a smaller, more family-like home. In 1966, we opened another house in Trosly, les Rameaux, where Steve and Ann Newroth welcomed three men from the Val, and in 1968, we opened l'Ermitage. In 1969, in the nearby town of Cuise we opened Valinos, where we welcomed ten women. Between 1970 and 1977 we opened the following houses: la Grande Source, la Petite Source and la Cascade in Trosly; la Nacelle and la Vigne in Breuil; la Promesse, la Manne and l'Olivier in Pierrefonds; a second home for women, Massabielle, in Cuise; and le Tremplin, l'Isba and Lalla Mariam in Compiègne. In 1968, we welcomed 73 people into our houses; in 1970, there were 112; in 1972, 126. At that time, some of those we welcomed had very slight handicaps. That is why we were able to help fourteen people (seven of whom

34

are married today) to live in their own apartments and find ordinary jobs.

The expansion in Trosly can be explained partly by the number of requests we received from parents, social workers, psychiatric hospitals and others, and partly by the financial encouragement (in terms of capital and running costs) that we received from the local government, which encouraged the creation of small homes for people with mental handicaps.

The number of assistants also increased. Many came after hearing my talks or following a retreat in Canada. Little by little assistants began to put down their roots. Between 1965 and 1972 we saw the arrival of Anne-Marie and Annie Morinvillé, Pierre Brunière, Barbara Swanekamp (1965); Françoise Lagand, Gilbert Adam, Charles Lucas (1966); Jeanne Riandey (1967); Marie-Elisabeth Rouchette, Anne-Marie Ortolo (1968); Odile Ceyrac, Fernand Tauleigne, Catherine David(1969); Antoinette Maurice, Josiane Gueusquin, Dominique Berthy (1970); Gary Webb, Françoise Cambier, Simone Landrien, Emmanuelle Wacrenier, Règine Petit (1971); Jean de la Selle, Claire de Miribel, Jacqueline Sacré, Alain Saint Macary (1972). The community was growing rather wildly without much vision or common reflection. It was still very much a time of foundation. We were doing things step by step; a house was for sale, we bought it and we filled it! We did not even ask if the house was properly adapted to the needs of those we were to welcome!

The community suffered from my absences. Everything was in my hands, yet I went to Canada every year for the months of February and August. In 1969, I started travelling to India, and then to Africa, Haiti and Latin America. Besides that, there were my regular absences for meetings and talks in France, as I was very involved in the social work sector of the region and gave courses in two schools for special educators. However, it was not until 1970 that the body of more committed assistants created the role of Deputy Director and asked Antoinette Maurice to take on the role. This enabled them to make decisions while I was away. In spite of all this, or perhaps because of all this, God continued to watch over us. Assistants assumed an enormous amount of work. I remember one workshop where there were twenty men and one assistant. It was a heroic time in our history.

The repercussions of my naiveté were felt in 1971, when a whole movement of opposition to L'Arche rose up in Trosly. It began with just a handful of people, but grew. They presented a petition against us to the local authorities. Some people in the village feared that we were going to take over the whole village and make it into a centre for people with handicaps. There was a positive side to the petition; it forced us to start a dialogue with the people of the village and sign a written agreement with them that we would not expand further. It was true that I was more concerned about the needs of those who had handicaps—many of whom were coming out of the psychiatric hospital in Clermont—than with the need to inform local people or work with them. This had led to a certain imbalance between the size of the village, Trosly, and the number of people we welcomed. There was a danger of creating another form of ghetto or "institution" where people with handicaps were separate from others. The village's small size helped us realize that, in fact, integration into the local community is one of L'Arche's objectives. Our community's role is to reveal to society and the church the human value and mission of people with handicaps; it cannot be achieved if the community is too big. The growth of the community has nevertheless had some advantages: it allowed the creation of a sort of "motherhouse" in L'Arche that can welcome and help in the formation of a number of assistants who can then go to communities in France or other countries. If L'Arche-Trosly had remained small and prophetic, we would never have been able to grow as we did in other parts of the world.

During all this time of growth in Trosly, and with my frequent trips abroad, Fr. Thomas' role was essential. While he did not want to be involved in running the community (although he did agree to be on the Community Council), he was there as a friend, a spiritual father, the priest for many in the community as well as in the village and surrounding area. He encouraged and supported them, celebrated eucharist, prayed and reassured those who were worried about what I was doing!

During this era, the Board of Directors followed me more or less enthusiastically. I also chaired the board (which is not generally done). This did, however, permit a certain unity between the community and the board. The Board of Directors was a place for discussion, discernment and control of our expansion. Some members of the Board, like Étienne Gout, the former director of Social Security in France, helped and supported me in an exceptional way. I was gradually beginning to understand the board's role and place in L'Arche. It was not just a necessary evil in order to have legal status, but an essential part of L'Arche. Its members could be real friends and full members of the community, bringing their competence, their questions, their share of the vision and their love to help the community grow and develop.

As the community grew, it also deepened. The Val Fleuri was gradually becoming a place of peace and of prayer, thanks to Odile and Gilbert who carried a lot during those difficult years. The large numbers of people at the Val decreased with the creation of new homes, and much was done to make it more like a home. In the Val, men like George and René Petit were able to grow in a special way in the love of Jesus.

## Expansion throughout France and in other countries

*La Merci*

When I took on the Val Fleuri in March 1965, I realized quickly that many of the men had no family and thus no place to go on holidays. I felt it was extremely important that we find a place to give them a change during the month of August. In 1966, while we were on our way to Fatima on pilgrimage, we visited the Carmelite sisters in Cognac. I thought to myself how good it would be to find a place near this Carmelite monastery, which could support the group through its prayers and love. The Carmelites and some friends arranged a meeting with people from the area; I told them of our idea. A few months later, in February 1967, Monique de Pracomtal called to tell me that a good house on a beautiful piece of land about 15 kilometers from Cognac was for sale for 40,000 French francs. The next day Jacqueline d'Halluin went down to see it; we had given her a blank cheque; she bought the house.

In August 1967, the first group from Trosly went to Cognac for their summer holiday. But even then we felt that we could not leave the house empty eleven months of the year. We tried to think of how it could be more useful throughout the year. Thus was born the idea of founding a new community. This idea became a more concrete reality when Agnès and Adriano da Silva, who had met at L'Arche in Trosly, decided to get married. I had met Adriano at my lectures in Canada and Agnès had attended talks I gave at a school for specialized educators directed by Dr. Préaut at Epinay; she came to the Val Fleuri as part of her practical training. Agnès and Adriano agreed to begin the new community. Alain de Pracomtal, Monique's husband, agreed to chair the local committee, which was an extension of the National Board of Directors.

In October 1969, la Merci opened its doors as a day workshop for people with mental handicaps. Then, in January 1970, the da Silvas opened their first home.

## Daybreak

Steve and Ann Newroth came to L'Arche in 1966; they opened our third home, les Rameaux. Steve was also responsible for a maintenance team that took care of the numerous repairs in the houses. They left Trosly in 1967 to attend the Ecumenical Institute in Boissy near Geneva for a year. When they returned to Toronto in 1969, they hoped to start a L'Arche community. What a joy it was for them when Sr. Rosemarie Donovan made it possible to begin by giving them her community's former novitiate house in Richmond Hill. A Board of Directors was set up and Daybreak, the first L'Arche community in North America, opened its doors in October, 1969.

## Asha Niketan, Bangalore

Perhaps the most amazing place of growth was in India, through Mira Ziauddin and Gabrielle Einsle. Mira, an Indian woman, is a friend of Louis Pretty. I met her in Montreal and she came to L'Arche in May 1965. Her father was Muslim and her mother Hindu. She had become a Catholic at the end of her studies and deeply desired a style of life close to the beatitudes. In 1969, when her father fell sick, she felt called to return to Madras to take care of him, but was torn between her father and L'Arche. There seemed to be only one solution: start a L'Arche community in Madras where she could also be close to her father. This foolish idea, which sprang up during a conversation with Mira, touched Gabrielle's heart as well. Gabrielle is a German woman who was then in charge of Crossroads, a centre for foreign students in Montreal, but yearned to go to India. Mira and Gabrielle had known each other in Montreal.

We had no funds and few contacts for such an adventure, but in February 1969, Roby Kidd, a member of Daybreak's board, put me in touch with General Spears of C.I.D.A. (Canadian International Development Agency). He was responsible for distributing government funds to volunteer agencies, especially in Third World countries. He informed me that money was available if we could present a project and a budget. So, Gabrielle and I went into a little restaurant, wrote up a project and invented a budget—without knowing anything about India. Within a few weeks we received a check for over C\$30,000. We were no longer faced with just a possibility: we had started a project and there was no turning back. I must say I was a little frightened.

Mira and Gabrielle went to Bangalore in October 1969. I joined them a month later. I had already been corresponding with Major Ramachandra, a disciple of Gandhi, who was keen to see that something be done in India for people with handicaps. When I arrived in Bangalore, a letter from him told me that he would be in Bangalore the following day.

When I met him, he told me of a property that he could let us have. I could hardly believe my ears. Gabrielle and I visited the property: a good house with two wells, just outside the city. I gave a few talks in Bangalore and asked those who seemed interested in L'Arche if they would form a board of directors for a future community. Thus, in October 1970, through a very obvious act of Providence, L'Arche in India, known as Asha Niketan (Home of Hope) opened its doors to people with handicaps.

The board we created in Bangalore was composed of Hindus and Christians. Because we would be welcoming assistants and handicapped people who were both Hindu and Christian, we had to write an inter-faith charter. Gabrielle and I wrote that charter; the Board worked on it again and then included it in the Society's legal statutes in order to specify the objectives of Asha Niketan and guarantee as much as

*Srinivas and Narasinga in Ashe Niketan, Bangalore*

possible its continuity in vision and spirit with that of L'Arche.

## Les Trois Fontaines

In 1969, I received a letter from Sr. Marie-Madeleine of the Carmelite Monastery in Abbeville. She told me of friends near Boulogne-sur-Mer who were willing to rent three properties to L'Arche on a long term basis for the symbolic sum of one franc. They would ask us simply to take on all the usual responsibilities that come with owning property. I went to visit the properties in Ambleteuse and quite soon afterwards they were ours. Fr. Thomas' brother, Joseph Philippe, an architect, agreed to renovate the buildings. The local authorities gave us the necessary funds and permission to start a centre.

Les Trois Fontaines began in 1971 with a small home, then gradually added a workshop and other homes. I met Marcelle Decroix, who was head of a school near Boulogne for children and adolescents with mental handicaps. She wanted to leave that job and agreed to take on the responsibility for this new L'Arche community.

*Little Ewell*

My sister, Thérèse, accompanied the Faith and Light pilgrims from England to Lourdes in 1971. At Lourdes she confided to me that she felt called to leave her role as a doctor in St. Thomas Hospital in London, and live more closely with the poor by starting a L'Arche community in England. We agreed that God would give us some signs or indications as to where it should be located. A little later, a woman wrote offering us a house in Canterbury. We could not take up that offer, but it did orient us towards the Canterbury area where, finally, with the support of the Archbishop of Canterbury, then Michael Ramsey, the legal society of L'Arche in the United Kingdom bought an old Anglican rectory in Barfrestone. The community of Little Ewell was born in 1974.

## The Federation, a place of unity

Up until then, all the communities had been founded by people who had personal relationships with me. The founders, however, did not know each other very well. There was no structure for mutual support or decision-making; there was no place to formulate a common vision. In 1972, all these founders met at Ambleteuse. It was the first meeting of what would later become the Federation of L'Arche. That first meeting brought together Fr. Thomas, myself, Marie-Hélène Mathieu (Board member of L'Arche-France), Agnès and Adriano da Silva (la Merci), Steve and Ann Newroth (Daybreak), Gabrielle Einsle (Asha Niketan), Marcelle

Decroix (les Trois Fontaines) and Thérèse Vanier (Little Ewell). We began by writing down the vision of L'Arche in a Charter, which for a long time was referred to as the "International Charter of L'Arche." We worked on the text again after that first meeting and made amendments. All the communities except Asha Niketan, Bangalore, which already had its own Charter, approved the final text of the Charter at the second Federation in 1973. At this first Federation, a small International Council was formed to accompany new foundations. The Council members were myself (International Coordinator), Marie-Hélène Mathieu (Vice-Coordinator), Steve Newroth, Agnès da Silva and Gabrielle Einsle.

*At top, Steve Newroth (with Frederick in his arms)*
*and Ann Newroth, along with other residents*
*of Daybreak, Richmond Hill, Ontario*

III

# GROWTH OF THE FAMILY
## (1972-1977)

### The Second and Third Federation meetings (1973, 1975)

After the Federation's first meeting in 1972, many other communities were born. The second Federation meeting took place in October 1973, eighteen months after the first one. Representatives from twelve communities attended, along with three observers. That meeting's goal was to help us get to know each other and give thanks for each other's presence in L'Arche. The meeting took place at three different sites: first in Little Ewell (England), then in L'Arche-Trosly, and finally in the Monastery of Ourscamp (15 kilometres from Trosly). During this meeting we confirmed the existence of two charters: the Indian Charter which, since 1970, had provided for inter-faith communities, and the Charter from the first Federation meeting, which was specifically Christian. We had decided not to try to agree on one Charter which, to be acceptable to everyone, would remain vague from a Christian point of view.

In 1975, the third Federation meeting was held at Shadow Lake, Canada. Representatives from twenty-six communities attended, plus five observers. We set up new structures to help maintain unity between communities, to give communities more adequate support, to prepare new foundations and to give general orientations. The delegates elected Sue Mosteller to replace me as International Coordinator. She chose as Vice-Coordinator Alain Saint Macary. The Federation was divided into regions, each with a coordinator: three North American regions (with coordinators Pat Lenon, George Strohmeyer and Brian Halferty, plus Steve Newroth as North American Coordinator); one region for the United Kingdom and Scandinavia (Thérèse Vanier); one region for France (Marie-Hélène Mathieu); one region for India (Gabrielle Einsle); and one region for Africa (Dawn Follett). So we now had an International Council composed of all the coordinators plus myself to watch over L'Arche's growth and spirit. It was the first step in decentralization, since each Regional Coordinator was now responsible for supporting the communities and following up new projects within his or her region. They were called to coordinate a Regional Council at which all the community leaders in the same region could meet, share together and find mutual support.

The first meeting of the International Council was held in Trosly in October 1975. We did not know quite what our role was. We discovered it together, with time and through various events. Throughout all that period, Sue was able to gain everyone's confidence and assume authority with competence and vision. At that particular moment of our history, she was clearly God's chosen instrument to help bring to birth the larger family of L'Arche.

The second meeting of the International Council was held in Bouaké (Ivory Coast) in April 1976, while I was in the hospital in Paris. We had chosen Bouaké as the meeting site because the new community there was going to have its official inauguration. Since we could not change the date because of the inauguration, the International Council met without me. Responsibilities in L'Arche were beginning to be shared.

Faced with all the requests from many groups and individuals who wanted to become or start a L'Arche community, the International Council wrote a document on new foundations. It proposed that the International Council first accept a new community for a probationary period of one year or more, followed by second step of final acceptance. This was approved and put into practice.

These structures (the International Council and the Regional Councils) have evolved over the years. They contained embryonic forms of our present structures. Gradually we understood that a community cannot manage on its own. It needs an external authority to help form the director in his or her role as shepherd. To begin with, the coordinators had the role of coordinating, as the name suggests. Little by little, because of difficulties and crises in communities, they were called to assume a role of authority. As the years have passed, we have seen the need for a support system to help communities grow, deepen and resolve crises.

It has taken us time to learn how to use our structures well, to discover what discernment is and how to make decisions in truth and with God's guidance. We have made mistakes, but we have forums where we can look at them, analyse them, understand them, and learn from them.

One of the graces of the Federation Meeting at Shadow Lake was a meeting with an Australian, Eileen Glass, who was a delegate from the Winnipeg community. She spoke with me about her desire to see L'Arche begin one day in her own country. I said that if God wanted L'Arche in Australia, I would be invited to give a retreat there. Two years later I received just such an invitation! Eileen was God's privileged instrument in founding L'Arche in Australia in 1978.

**Foundations**

New communities continued to spring up. These foundations were quite fragile. Directors had little support. Everything was done with much generosity and a real desire to follow Jesus, and to follow the signs of Providence. There was the same sense of urgency to get people with handicaps out of big institutions and to bring them the good news of God's love. There was the same desire to create alternative communities that were well integrated into society. These years were marked by a new hope born of the second Vatican Council. They were also characterized by a certain intolerance towards old ways of doing things: for example, state or church institutions were seen as fortresses of power, security and certainty, far from the insecurity and the poverty of the gospel, and far from the cry of the poor in the world. The L'Arche foundations from that era were the fruits of a changing world and of a church seeking new ways of living and announcing the good news. It was a church that was seeking new paths, closer to the poor in many ways, even though in many ways it was set rigidly in traditions and institutions dictated by its past history.

## North America

Communities in North America were either born out of a Faith and Sharing Retreat or established by people sent from Daybreak. Judie Leckie was sent to Vancouver by the Daybreak Community to start the new community of Shiloah in a large house loaned to L'Arche by the United Church of Canada; Marjorie Pickersgill was sent to Stratford to start a community in a house given to L'Arche by a Catholic parish; Brian and Mary Lou Halferty left Daybreak to start L'Arche Frontenac on a property they had bought.

Generally, communities that were born during those six years were linked to two models. Some were modelled after L'Arche-Trosly and Daybreak; they wanted to be Christian communities centred on the poor. They were financed, supported and controlled by government agencies and they wanted to work with professionals. They had solid Boards of

Directors. Other communities wanted to be closer to the poor by living the insecurity of the poor and refusing all state aid and control. They were integrated into poor neighbourhoods in large cities or in the country close to the land; often they welcomed other marginal people besides people with mental handicaps.

The majority of the communities, even if their orientations were slightly different, welcomed people from large institutions, many of whom were quite disturbed after spending a number of years separated from their family environment. Although some communities suffered from difficult situations because of this, it is also true that many men and women from these institutions made real passages from death to life, from anguish to trust.

North America is a vast continent. The distance between communities is great; each community has its own Board of Directors. That is why there was so little contact between them, at least until 1975. Each one developed along its own lines with little common vision or orientation.

### Belgium

Fr. André Roberti started le Toit in Brussels in 1971 to provide a home for a few men and women who had cerebral palsy. They participated in the Faith and Light pilgrimage to Lourdes at Easter 1971. There Fr. Roberti came to know L'Arche. In 1973, he asked the general assembly of delegates at the second Federation of L'Arche if le Toit could be part of L'Arche. His request was accepted. Fr. Roberti facilitated the first foundations in Belgium, which were all administered by the National Board of Directors in Brussels.

Le Toit's special gift was the great openness of its welcome. The community lived in great poverty, without any government aid; assistants had to work outside the community, at least half-time, in order to pay for their room and board. Little by little, le Toit discovered the specific call of L'Arche: to welcome people with mental handicaps.

## France

Like Belgium, France had a National Board with local committees that were close to the communities. Most of the new foundations that began when a property was given to L'Arche were modelled after L'Arche-Trosly and received a government grant from the government. Two communities, however, Moita and la Rebellerie (founded after 1978) chose not to ask for government aid in the beginning, but to be self-supporting. They lived on money from their own work on the land or from the allowances and salaries of people with handicaps and assistants, who had to find work outside the community.

## The United Kingdom

Communities in the United Kingdom were founded and developed according to the model of L'Arche-Trosly. They received government grants, and had Boards of Directors and local committees close to each of the communities. In general, they had excellent professional support, but sometimes lacked spiritual support, perhaps because of their ecumenical vocation. These communities welcomed both men and women with mental handicaps and assistants from different traditions. Little by little, they helped us discover the gift of ecumenism. L'Arche did not set out to be ecumenical; rather, it was gifted with this calling.

## Scandinavia

Father Jorgen Hviid established Niels Steenssens Hus in Denmark after the Faith and Light pilgrimage. Wera Saether established Maria Huset shortly afterwards in Norway. The two communities found it difficult to grow and get established in the social and ecclesial context of these countries.

*Haiti, Africa, India and Honduras*

After the founding of Asha Niketan in India, some people yearned to see L'Arche in Africa. Dawn Follett and Françoise Cambier went to visit three African countries: Burkina Faso, Ivory Coast and the Cameroons. They met with religious groups, government authorities and social service organizations in each country to evaluate the needs and the possibility of setting up a L'Arche community. A small group was ready to start this new foundation: Dawn, and Gus and Debby Leuschner. After much prayer and reflection, we decided it should begin in Bouaké, Ivory Coast. One of the major factors in this decision was the presence of a monastery of Benedictines who, with their prior, Fr. Denis Martin, encouraged us to come, and promised their help and support.

Dawn, Gus and Debby arrived in Bouaké in 1974; a few months later they had a rented home to which they welcomed Ngoran and Seydoux from the local psychiatric centre. L'Arche Bouaké was born.

In 1969, Sr. Micheline Vinet attended one of the retreats I gave in Ottawa. Soon afterwards, she was sent to Haiti. As she had been deeply touched by the retreat, she yearned to have the same type of retreat for people in Haiti. In 1974, Fr. Jacques Beaudry invited me to give a retreat in the Foyer de Charité at Port-au-Prince. The following year I returned to Haiti, this time with Robert Larouche who had been in Trosly for a year. Robert felt a call to begin L'Arche in Haiti. Fr. Beaudry gave him much support and encouragement. In July 1975, Robert was able to welcome Jolibois, Yveline and Jean-Robert. The adventure of L'Arche in Haiti had begun.

When Robert and I went to Haiti in 1975, Nadine Tokar, who had been with L'Arche in Trosly since 1972, came with us. After the retreat, we went together to Brazil where I gave a retreat to a group of Canadian missionaries. As the result of the talks we gave there, Faith and Light communities were born. Much later, in 1987, they gave birth to a L'Arche community in Sao Paolo.

On the return flight to France, Nadine confided to me that she felt very drawn to Honduras. At that time I didn't know anything about that country. Neither did Nadine. She admits now that she doesn't really know why she said it. Mysteriously enough, a few weeks later I received a letter from the Bishop of Choluteca in Honduras asking me to come and give a retreat to his priests. I immediately called Nadine and said, "I think Jesus heard what you said on the plane!" In February 1976, Nadine and I went to Choluteca and Tegucigalpa where I gave retreats. A year later, Nadine moved into Nueva Suyapa, a slum area in the suburbs of Tegucigalpa. She was warmly welcomed into the home of Dona Maria and Don Umberto—a shack made of wooden planks. While there, she contacted the San Felipe Asylum as well as various families in the neighbourhood to discover the needs of people with mental handicaps. A year later, the parish priest of Suyapa offered her a small house that had been the parish school. Nadine moved in and welcomed Lita from the neighbourhood and Marcia from San Felipe Asylum. She also made the contacts necessary to welcome Rafael, whom she had found completely abandoned in a Tegucigalpa hospital.

All these communities had clearly chosen to be integrated into poor neighbourhoods and to welcome people who had been totally abandoned. As these countries have fewer rules and restrictions, it was easier for our communities to welcome both children and adults into the same home. This gave these communities a very particular character.

In India, other Asha Niketans were opened.

The communities in Haiti, the Ivory Coast, Honduras and India brought much to the Federation as a whole. They reminded us of the value of simplicity, welcome and sharing. They also reminded us of the danger of wealth and individualism in our richer countries and helped us recognize that solidarity goes deeper than financial assistance.

## The role of Providence

The hand of God was clearly present at the foundation of each of these communities—and that is still true today. God continued to watch over us throughout these years. When I think of those foundations, I see how everything was given: a sign or a gift led us to another sign, another gift. It was as if we were walking on a road without knowing quite where it was leading. We were sure that it was leading somewhere and that it was all in God's plan of love for the poor and the weak. I have truly experienced that if we put everything into God's hands and try to follow the signs, things will evolve peacefully.

At the same time, we were inexperienced and did not realize all that a new foundation needed. I was quite idealistic. And, no doubt, I also needed to prove something, and had real difficulty waiting for the right moment, the moment chosen by God. We made errors; we will talk about them later. Perhaps I had to experience these mistakes in order to learn better how to act according to God's ways. My faith was real, but I lacked a certain understanding and the consistency necessary to truly help the new communities grow and develop. I could not give them the support they needed. The first founding directors, like myself, lacked experience and an understanding of what L'Arche was. I'm always amazed to see how God made use of each one of us with our qualities and faults. He did not wait until we were perfect. Despite many errors in those early days of L'Arche, God watched over each of the foundations, and some of those that got off to a bad start are full of life today.

## The search for our identity

*What models?*

One of the big difficulties facing all these foundations was the lack of a single, clear model of what a L'Arche community should be.

The first community in Trosly was, in the beginning, quite marginal and prophetic. Then, with the arrival of le Val, it was integrated into the structures of France, while still keeping its prophetic element. Many of the other founders of the L'Arche communities had not received their formation in the first community. They did not know what L'Arche was.

During the 1960's and 1970's, there were three different models of community life: religious communities such as the Missionaries of Charity, the Brothers of St. John, Taizé, etc.; group homes for people with handicaps that were developing in the United States, Canada, the United Kingdom and Scandinavia, with reintegration as their professional goal; and finally, new forms of community which, especially in North America, were reacting against the consumer society, big, depersonalized institutions and legal rigidity. Among these were The Catholic Worker, Friendship House and Benedict Labre House. Others wanted to live close to the earth, others were "communes" that wanted to live simply and poorly, and sometimes close to the poor—without all the constraints of society. Many of these communities were too idealistic and did not last long.

You find elements of these three models in the different L'Arche foundations of that time. Some tended towards the professional model, others towards the religious model, and still others chose the model of new communities close to the land and the poor. These new L'Arche foundations suffered from our lack of clarity about our identity. Only with time have we clarified and deepened it.

What was clear, however, from the very beginning was the aspect of "living with" people who have a mental handicap, a desire to create family with them. We also knew that this "living with" could not be accomplished without God's help. The two pillars of L'Arche are the poor, with whom we want to share our lives, and God, who alone can transform and heal our hearts.

However, we still had a great deal to learn in our communities. In the beginning, most of us had no real sense of the role and place of a board, priests and ministers, or professionals. We were not articulating our spirituality clearly or indicating what we needed to nurture it. We had no idea of the complexity of the communities whose vocation was ecumenical or inter-faith. L'Arche was trying to find its way. I think it was precisely this lack of clarity about L'Arche's vision and the new foundations' needs that caused serious crises and deep suffering in certain communities.

## Broadening my vision

During the years of expansion, through my lectures and retreats in Canada, the Faith and Light pilgrimage and the explosion that afterwards led to the birth of many Faith and Light communities throughout the world, my consciousness of world realities gradually began to change.

My trips to India that began in 1969 deeply marked my life. I discovered a whole world of poverty that I had never seen before in my life. At the time of the Civil War in Bangladesh, I visited Calcutta and met Mother Teresa and her sisters; hundreds of thousands of refugees were flooding into India. As I walked the streets, I saw so many men, women and children lying there. I visited areas of extreme poverty and centres for people suffering from leprosy.

In India, I also discovered the vision and work of Mahatma Gandhi, especially his spirituality. In him I found a prophet for our times, a man of God, a man of prayer, a man deeply concerned about the life of the poor who saw the "untouchables" as *harijans*, children of God. Gandhi was concerned with peace and unity, a man ready to risk his life in non-violence, which for him was a spiritual reality rather than a political one. This man had a whole vision of the land, of villages, life and manual work which was quite different from that of our modern society. Gandhi marked my life deeply; he opened my mind and enlarged my consciousness.

I was also beginning to discover the Ivory Coast, Haiti and Honduras. These countries were so different from the rich, comfortable cultures of the West. This made me realize more than ever the ugliness and sinfulness of materialism and individualism in richer countries.

Around the same time, in 1973, I began to make contact with prisons in Canada where I gave talks and retreats. I met the world of juvenile delinquency and crime. In these prisons, I met many broken men and women whose self-images were wounded. The terrible sufferings of their childhoods had affected their psychological, moral and spiritual development. During my talks I would tell them about the suffering that men and women in L'Arche had known: rejection, abandonment, anguish and all the forces of violence and deprivation they had experienced in large psychiatric hospitals or asylums. Through all that, I was actually describing what they themselves had lived and suffered.

I began to see more clearly how our societies are divided. On the one hand, there are the "rich," the satisfied, the secure who are locked up in themselves, and in a world of fear, security and superficialities. On the other hand are the "poor," who, although dissatisfied with their lot and locked up in anger and depression, are often more open to hear and receive the good news of Love. The hearts of the poor are often more broken than their bodies.

And so I began to discover the gospel's deeper meaning, how it is truly "good news" for the poor. The gospel and the words and gestures of Jesus ruled my life and enlightened my understanding and faith more and more. The poor are a sign, a presence of Jesus. God chose what was foolish and weak in the eyes of the world to shame the wise and the strong. He chose what was lowest and most despised. To truly accept this message of the poor as a sign and presence of God, we need to accept our own poverty; we must let Jesus and his Holy Spirit touch and transform us through prayer.

These contacts with the different worlds of poverty affirmed and broadened my vision of L'Arche as a gospel-based community. I saw the person before I saw his or her poverty. And I realized that the person who is hungry, abandoned or in need is first of all a heart who needs to find another heart; someone who will listen, understand and love. People who are poor and discouraged need to hear someone say to them, "I love you. I have confidence in you. You are beautiful. You can give life to others." This helps them find new confidence in themselves, new strength, new hope. The poor do not need to hear a lot of words, not even pious words. They may need people who will do things for them. Above all they need friendship: friends who love them and are willing to do things with them. This will help them grow and develop both humanly and spiritually.

In 1954, I had met the Little Sisters of Jesus in Montreal, in particular, Little Sister Monique, whose sister, Anne-Marie de la Selle, has been in L'Arche-Trosly since 1968. Over the years, L'Arche and the Little Sisters and Little Brothers of Jesus have come to know each other better. We have discovered that we have a common spirituality of humility and presence, close to the poor and the weak; a common call to live with them, not to change them, but to welcome them and share their gifts and their beauty; to discover in them the presence of Jesus—Jesus, humble and gentle, Jesus, poor and rejected. It is the spirituality of Nazareth: to live daily life simply and humbly, with love: to be present to the poor. I was beginning to discover the spirituality of L'Arche.

My own experience of sickness strengthened this vision of the poor at the heart of L'Arche and at the heart of the church. On my return from India in 1976, I fell sick and had to be hospitalized. I had some intestinal infection, but above all, I was completely exhausted. Two months of impoverishment due to illness taught me a great deal. Jesus used this time to renew me spiritually. It was also an invitation for me to rest, and to pay more attention to my body and the pace of my life. After that period of illness, I made two retreats with Fr. Marie-Dominique Philippe in Chateauneuf de Galaure. I discovered the charism of the Foyers de Charité and of Marthe Robin who carried L'Arche in her heart and prayers.

### "La Ferme"

In 1973, Fr. Thomas left the sacristy near the old chapel and moved into the group of buildings called "la Ferme." Many people from outside L'Arche came there for a retreat with Fr. Thomas or just for a few days' rest and prayer. Assistants from Trosly and from other communities also came to find rest and prayer. Little by little La Ferme became a spiritual centre at the heart of the community, where Fr. Thomas would give spiritual guidance and talks on theology. There was also a place of silent prayer, the oratory, where the Blessed Sacrament was exposed throughout the day.

La Ferme has played an important, though hidden, role in the development of L'Arche. In some way, it has been a model for the houses of prayer that have come to birth in other L'Arche communities. It is a place where we can get away from the noise and activity of community life to meet Jesus in the silence of our own hearts and let him renew us.

### Normalization

In 1971 and 1972, through Steve Newroth, I became acquainted with the Scandinavian vision of people with mental handicaps and the theory of normalization. Steve had introduced me to Wolf Wolfensberger, a man who fought a great deal for the recognition of the rights of handicapped people in the United States; he spoke against the existing attitudes and structures of oppression which operate against them.

There is something very beautiful in the theory of normalization: people with mental handicaps are complete human beings who have rights like every other human being; they should be welcomed into society on an equal basis; they should be allowed to go to the local swimming pool, movies, churches, just like anyone else. They should even be able to go to school with all the other children. It is tragic when people with handicaps are excluded. Exclusion results in a broken self-image, anguish and, ultimately, a sense of guilt. Everything must be done to help people with handicaps have confidence in themselves, sense their own human dignity and develop their manual and intellectual capacities to the fullest.

That theory is rich and true. In North America, people were enthusiastic about it, and I learned a great deal from them. Were we in L'Arche too protective? Did we place enough trust in our people and their capacity to grow towards greater independence and renewed dignity? Was there not a danger in the gospel vision of over-identifying the poor with people who have handicaps, spiritualizing their needs for growth too quickly, deifying their poverty? This would not help them progress to greater freedom. Love should never be opposed to the competence necessary for the development of each person's potential.

But isn't there another danger in taking normalization to an extreme? When our societies speak of "normality," do they really identify it with what is most deeply human? Are our societies truly human? Are they not rather pushing us towards extreme individualism, infidelity in relationships

and the primacy of pleasure and economics? Maybe normalization does not sufficiently consider the deepest needs of
persons with handicaps and the special gifts they give to
society. Their affectivity is rich, spontaneous and true; they
are constant reminders of the values of the heart in a society
that tends to exalt competence and efficiency and forget
love. The cry for community from people with handicaps
constantly reminds us that we all need community. While it
is true that people with handicaps are called to develop and
grow towards greater autonomy, they need above all a whole
network of friendships and a community that gives them
security and a sense of belonging, awakens each one's gifts,
encourages growth, and develops love and a sense of service.

# IV

---

# GROWTH IN MATURITY

## (1978-1982)

### The Fourth Federation Meeting
### (Chateauneuf de Galaure, France, 1978)

The Federation meeting in 1978 marked a new, important period in the history of L'Arche: it was a time of greater maturity. Even though new communities were still coming to birth, it was no longer a time of expansion but rather, a time of deepening and structuring. L'Arche was becoming more conscious of its own identity, spirituality and call. To be able to live and deepen our lives in L'Arche, to be able to hold our own in a materialistic and individualistic culture in which the weak are ignored and rejected, we had to find the right structures and a solid, clear support system for the communities. An authentic community life is difficult, if not impossible, without good support and spiritual nourishment.

The meeting in Chateauneuf provided us with an opportunity for us to grasp more fully a sense of the larger, international family of L'Arche. Forty-nine communities were represented.

The organization of this meeting was quite different from that at Shadow Lake. The meeting was divided into two parts. The first part, in which board members and community leaders participated, was more verbal and intellectual. The second part, in which assistants and people with handicaps participated, was more festive. We discovered, however, that it was not necessarily a good thing to bring Shyam from Bangalore for such a meeting. He suffered from the cold and did not appreciate French camembert at all! And Kuagio, from Bouaké, was so homesick—and discovered French wine and its effects! The culture shock was too great. We decided that in the future we would invite people with handicaps to regional and national meetings rather than to international ones.

While board members and community leaders were meeting together, assistants and people with handicaps were invited to visit our various European communities. In this way each of the European communities participated in the meeting. Communities forged links with each other. At the meeting itself, small groups helped people get to know others from different communities. Talks, time to experience different kinds of manual work from our workshops and times of celebration, like the celebration of the history of L'Arche and the final send-off, were included. There were also important times for prayer and eucharist. It was truly a time of celebration for the L'Arche family.

We greatly appreciated the presence of board members. This meeting helped us to see their role and their place in L'Arche more clearly. Over those eight days together, we realized that they were full members of our communities and how much each of our communities needed their commitment, wisdom and competence. We realized how much they, too, are called to belong to the community and find spiritual nourishment in and through it.

### Nourishment

In 1978, we began to see the fruits of the International Council meetings. They gave us a greater sense of the needs of our communities on a global basis, especially the needs of our community leaders and long-term assistants. The Holy

Spirit was gradually helping us to see the need for formation programs, and for spiritual and intellectual nourishment.

*Renewals*

In 1979, in Wadderton England, we had the first English Renewal with about thirty assistants who had at least five years experience in L'Arche. They lived together for ten weeks of community life and prayer, with talks on such subjects as the cry of the poor, stages in human growth, family and community, signs of hope and peace in the world, and the vision and vocation of L'Arche. The International Council realized that it is important for the spiritual growth of each one and for the unity of the wider family of L'Arche to have these ten weeks of deepening together with people from different communities. Each one had time to re-read his or her past history and deepen his or her specific vocation in L'Arche. At the heart of the Renewal was a one-week silent retreat.

Since 1978, there has been a Renewal almost every year, either in English or in French. Many assistants admit that, if they are still in L'Arche today, it is because of this time away, these ten weeks of prayer, reflection and individual accompaniment by a priest and/or an older assistant in L'Arche. These Renewals are a time to deepen our vision of L'Arche intellectually, but more importantly, to deepen our spiritual life, our life of prayer in L'Arche.

These times of renewal have encouraged us to set up other formation programs to help assistants who have been in L'Arche for less than five years deepen their vision of L'Arche and learn certain practical things—like how to be a good house leader. In many Regions, mini-renewals are also held for assistants who have been in L'Arche two or three years. Most Regions now also have five-day retreats for assistants in their first year in L'Arche.

Some assistants living in different communities wanted to follow Jesus more closely, live more deeply in conformity with the gospel, make a public commitment to their call and their commitment to Jesus hidden in the poor, and offer one another more support. Robert Larouche from L'Arche-Haiti brought up this question of affirming our commitment. In March 1977, he wrote a letter to all our communities, asking if other assistants felt this same call and the need to affirm it. He received many positive responses. So a retreat was organized for those who could come. It was held in France, just before the 1978 Federation meeting, and was given by Fr. Marie-Dominique Philippe, a Dominican priest who is Fr. Thomas' brother.

Thirty people from different communities attended that retreat. It was like a little Pentecost! The question came up: "How can we express our commitment towards the people who have been entrusted to us?" I spoke to Fr. Marie-Dominique about this. I told him I did not feel that "vow" was the right word for us, but that when I reflected on what I was living with Raphaël and Philippe, the word which came to mind was "covenant." I felt that it was a question, not simply of my commitment towards Raphaël and Philippe, but also of the reciprocity between us. They had something to give me that I was called to receive. God had bonded us together.

As a theologian, Fr. Marie-Dominique took up this notion and explained it. That is how the idea of covenant was born during that retreat. Some of those present said that they felt ready to make a public commitment to this covenant between themselves and Jesus, and those Jesus had entrusted to them. At the end of the retreat, during eucharist, just before communion, and in front of all who were present, we affirmed the bond, the covenant that Jesus had established between our hearts and the hearts of the poor. Fr. Marie-Dominique called by name each one of those who wished to

*Raphaël Simi with Jean*

affirm this covenant and said, "You are invited to live a covenant in L'Arche, with Jesus and with all your brothers and sisters, especially the poorest and the weakest. Do you want this?" Each one answered, "Yes."

Those who lived the retreat experienced it as a true time of grace. Evidently the Holy Spirit had inspired and guided everything. Our hearts were at peace and full of deep joy. However, in our naiveté, we had not considered how those who had not been at the retreat—and they were many— would react! Many had not been free to come. They did not understand this new form of commitment. They were hurt by being left out of this new, unexpected step, and feared that we were trying to create an elite in L'Arche. The pain and misunderstandings which followed that retreat lasted several years.

These difficulties, however, obliged those who had said yes to a covenant to look more deeply into its spiritual and theological meaning and implications. It is an affirmation before brothers and sisters that Jesus is calling us to discover his presence in the poor and to grow in God's love through our bonds with them. Each one, of course, lives this bond differently. Those who accept celibacy in view of the kingdom live it differently from those who are married; those who live full-time in the community live it differently from friends and Board members.

Later on, the International Council named a Covenant Commission to organize future retreats and clarify with theologians the notion of covenant and its implications. Since that first retreat in 1978, there have been many other Covenant retreats; over four hundred people have affirmed their covenant with Jesus and the poor in L'Arche.

The first Covenant retreats were held in the context of the Roman Catholic Church, as all the participants were Roman Catholic. In 1986, in England, the first Covenant retreat was organized in an ecumenical context. During the preparation for that retreat, we reflected on how we should celebrate the covenant in that context. We did not feel that it was appropriate to celebrate it during a eucharist in which everyone could not participate fully. We preferred to affirm the covenant during a liturgy centred on the word of God, the renewal of our baptismal vows and the washing of feet which, in St. John's gospel, replaces the account of the institution of the eucharist.

The following year, in April 1987, during the Covenant retreat which preceded the Federation meeting, some of our Hindu brothers from Asha Niketan wished to affirm their covenant with the poor in L'Arche. We adapted the liturgy of the washing of feet by adding sacred texts from Hindu scriptures, inviting each to express his or her faith in God at the time when Christians would renew their baptismal vows, and modifying the covenant formula for them: "You are invited to live a Covenant of love with God, in L'Arche, with your brothers and sisters, especially the poorest and the weakest. Do you want this?"

We see clearly what a gift of God the word "covenant" has been for us, and how it expresses the spiritual reality we are living in different cultural and religious contexts.

## *Retreats and renewals for people with handicaps*

The retreats and renewals organized for assistants led us gradually to see the necessity of organizing similar retreats and renewals adapted to the needs of people with handicaps.

In 1980, the first retreat for people with handicaps took place in France at the Foyer de Charité in Tressaint. Now almost every region has the same kind of retreat, for about thirty people, fifteen people with handicaps and their companions. These retreats are a time of grace, not only for people with handicaps but also for the assistants. The latter find that in these retreats the heart of L'Arche is revealed to them: not only do people with mental handicaps understand the message of the gospel, but they often live it at a deeper level than the assistants. These retreats have revealed to us the truth of the words of Jesus: "I thank you, Father, Lord of heaven and earth, because you have hidden these things from the wise and the intelligent and have revealed them to infants" (Matthew 11:25). People with mental handicaps know what it means to be a friend of Jesus, to trust him, to give him their hearts, to love him and be loved by him.

In 1981, the first renewal for people with handicaps, organized by the Great Lakes Region, took place in St. Joseph's College in Toronto. There were thirty participants: fifteen people with handicaps, each accompanied by an assistant from his/her community. Since then, several other renewals have been organized in other regions. The renewals, which are prepared long in advance, are a privileged moment when each person can tell his or her story and speak about intimate things: relationships with parents, the reality and pain of handicaps, experiences in the psychiatric hospital or in institutions, etc. These renewals have proven to be important moments of healing.

## Accompaniment

*The need*

One of L'Arche's great challenges is to find a way to nourish and sustain assistants in their vocation, so that they can put down permanent roots in L'Arche. The need for this personal accompaniment, especially spiritual accompaniment, was manifested quite quickly in L'Arche. However, it became an integral part of our community life only after the experience of the first renewals and retreats.

There is such a gap between a life of work and studies in society, with all the leisure activities and friendships that it implies, and community life with the poor, with all the loss of personal freedom and space, and the stress and demands that it involves. For assistants to make this passage and put down roots in community, they need much support and personal accompaniment.

It is fairly easy to live for a year or two in L'Arche. Many young people are capable, for example, of doing their national service in L'Arche. This calls for a certain amount of courage, energy and generosity. Many may have a high ideal of poverty and sharing their life for a limited period of time. But the question is: how do we help people put down life-long roots in a community where they are called to share their lives with people with handicaps?

During the first years in the history of L'Arche, several communities faced extremely difficult situations: they had welcomed men and women who had just come from long years in a psychiatric hospital. Their pain and suffering was enormous. And so, before anything else, we had to seek help from professional people. We had to respond to the needs of those who were quite disturbed. Often, in those first years, priests and ministers had trouble understanding L'Arche and seeing it as a new type of Christian community. They regarded us as just one more group home. This meant that during those first years of our existence many communities received little or no spiritual support. Assistants could not put down roots in the community in a permanent way.

The people with handicaps suffer when there is a shortage of assistants who can put down their roots in community. It is hard for the men and women in our homes to see someone they have come to love go away; it is particularly painful if that person is leaving to marry someone else from the community.

*Three types of accompaniment*

Over the years we have discovered three types of accompaniment—three ways to journey with assistants to support them:

(i) *In the workplace* One of the community leaders helps the assistant fulfill the assigned task. We all need to learn how to do a specific job and to be accountable to others for it.

(ii) *In the community* A more experienced assistant in L'Arche helps the assistant put down roots in this new culture, community life. When assistants first arrive in the community, they lose their former reference points; they leave their family, their circle of friends and their culture. They begin to discover the fears, wounds, fatigue and darkness within them. They need to find the right nourishment to give them the needed energy to befriend people with handicaps. They need someone who sees them not in terms of specific jobs or roles in the community, but as persons; someone who can help them grow in the path of love and gift of self.

(iii) *In the spiritual life* A spiritual guide helps the assistant re-read his or her past life, discover God's call, and deepen their life of communion and prayer with God.

When L'Arche first began, Fr. Thomas did this type of accompaniment. With the growth of L'Arche, more and more priests who were involved with our communities gave this individual, spiritual guidance. One of the first to come to L'Arche after Fr. Thomas was Bill Clarke, a Canadian Jesuit. He came to Trosly in 1968 to write a thesis on L'Arche as a new form of Christian community. This thesis, which was never completed, was published as a book, *Enough Room for Joy* (Toronto: McClelland & Stewart, 1974). It helped L'Arche become better known, especially in North America. Bill became a friend and a brother to us. He was able to articulate L'Arche's spirituality and affirm it publicly in covenant retreats in North America, Europe, Africa, Haiti and Honduras. He became the spiritual father to many assistants rooted in L'Arche. Bill was one of the first Jesuits to come to us who believed in L'Arche's mission. Later on, many others came to stay with us for longer or shorter periods. The Jesuits have a particular charism for giving individual retreats and accompanying people in their spiritual journey. Many communities and assistants have been deeply nourished, sustained, enlightened, guided and affirmed by Jesuit priests.

Every year since 1978, Fr. André de Jaer, a Belgian Jesuit, has organized a tertianship program in Trosly for about six Jesuits from different countries. (A tertianship program is the final stage of a Jesuit's training. It includes a long, silent retreat, studies of the documents and constitutions of the Society of Jesus, and supervised pastoral activity.) In this case, the Jesuits spend six months in the L'Arche community. Their presence as priests, as "companions of Jesus," who have no role of authority, has been a great help to us in our homes and workshops. In them we now have real friends in countries throughout the world. Because Fr. André has been in Trosly for the tertianship program, he has also been available to accompany assistants on their spiritual journey, give them eight-day or thirty-day retreats and help them discover and deepen their vocation in L'Arche.

Fortunately today, many priests, ministers and lay people with appropriate formation believe in the mission and vocation of L'Arche and can guide assistants spiritually. With the growth of L'Arche we still need many more!

## Welcoming people with severe handicaps

In 1978, we opened a new house in Trosly, la Forestière, where we welcomed Eric, Yvan, Edith, Marie-Jo and six others. Each one had severe mental handicaps; none of them could talk and their independence was very limited. I had started L'Arche with people who had a certain independence: they could work in the workshops. A few even left to live independently in their own apartments in Compiègne. As group homes and workshops organized by various Parents' Associations began to develop in France, we began to realize the pain and rejection of those who were more severely handicapped. They were too limited to fit into a workshop program or be welcomed into group homes. La Forestière brought a whole new dimension to L'Arche: the discovery of the presence of God hidden in the hearts of those who are extremely poor and weak.

I had carried this project to welcome people with severe handicaps in my heart for a long time. My very first plan was grandiose: eight buildings on the edge of Trosly, where we would welcome eighty people! Thanks be to God we never carried it out. The group of permanent assistants met, talked about this plan and rejected it. They proposed a more modest one that would allow better integration into the life of the existing community: one house in Trosly (la Forestière), and one in Cuise or Pierrefonds.

In 1980, when I left the responsibility as leader of the Trosly community, I asked Odile, who replaced me as Director, and the community council, if I could live and work

71

for a year at La Forestière. That year with Eric, Lucien and the others was important for me. I discovered the great capacity for relationship of these men and women who were very limited on the rational and verbal level. They were extremely poor intellectually, but tremendously rich in qualities of the heart. For us to perceive all the treasure of their hearts, we ourselves must become poor; we have to move into a slower pace of life, be more attentive, more centred and more contemplative. They invite us to an interior silence in order to welcome them within their silence.

After sixteen years of responsibility in the community and on the international level, I had to let go of my desires for efficiency and learn how to "waste time" in simple, loving relationships. I learned a great deal during that year, and my heart was transformed. I rediscovered the deep meaning of L'Arche. I also touched the powers of darkness hidden within my heart and experienced more deeply my own poverty. When we live day after day with people who are severely handicapped, our own limits and darkness become so obvious. But this experience helped me understand that we cannot grow in love and compassion unless, in all truth, we recognize who we are and accept our own radical poverty. The poor person is not just in others, but also within us. That truth is the basis of all human and spiritual growth and the foundation of our Christian life. "Blessed are the poor in spirit, for theirs is the kingdom of heaven" (Matthew 5:3). The poor, who reveal our poverty to us, thus become a sacrament.

### Links with the Roman Catholic Church

*The beginning*

L'Arche was founded through the inspiration and support of Fr. Thomas, who encouraged me to risk welcoming Raphaël and Philippe. His presence as a priest and his spiritual accompaniment with the sacrament of reconciliation and daily eucharist permitted people with handicaps, assistants, friends and the community as a whole to grow and deepen their spirituality. As a priest and a theologian, Fr. Thomas was both rigorous and open. He was deeply anchored in the traditions of the Roman Catholic Church, and also profoundly mystical. He blended fidelity to traditional values with an openness to the gift of the present moment.

When Bishop Desmazières was named Bishop of Beauvais in 1965, I went to see him, to tell him about L'Arche and about my desire to be in communion with him. Although there was no formal link between L'Arche and Bishop Desmazières, his friendship, visits and interest in our experience at L'Arche touched and encouraged me. They were a sign of our communion with the church.

During one of his visits to Trosly, I suggested that he come and live with us when he retired. A few years later, he reminded me of what I had said. In 1979, he left Beauvais and moved into a small house in Trosly; he became part of the team of assistants at l'Ermitage, where he ate all his meals. His presence was a source of grace for that house and the whole community. In 1981, at the age of 78, he went off like Abraham to found, with Alain Gsell, a new L'Arche community, Aigrefoin, near Paris.

Whenever there was a new foundation, one of the first things I always did was to inform the local bishop of our project and express our desire to be in communion with him. Each time the bishop welcomed us, showed real interest in L'Arche and promised his support. Sometimes he would express this in a very concrete way. In Calcutta, for example, the bishop offered us a rectory near Sealdah Station for the new community.

Priests founded some communities: Fr. André Roberti (le Toit); Fr. Jorgen Hviid (Nil Steensen Hus); Fr. George Strohmeyer (the Hearth); Fr. David Rothrock (Tahoma Hope); Fr. Peter Toohey (L'Arche Sydney). Priests fostered other communities, like la Corolle. The International Council has always insisted, however, that priest-founders gradually leave their role of responsibility so that they can live their priesthood more fully in the community and be men of prayer, rooted in the sacraments and the eucharist, close to the weakest and the poorest members and be wise spiritual guides.

## *The ordination of Gilbert Adam and Marc Prunier*

In 1978, Bishop Desmazières ordained two L'Arche assistants as priests, Gilbert Adam and Marc Prunier. For both this was the fulfilment of several years of theological and spiritual preparation, in addition to training periods at the seminary in Reims and the parishes of Clermont and Chantilly. After ordination, Gilbert stayed in Trosly and Marc went to la Merci. Both had been ordained for L'Arche, with ministries in the diocese. Gilbert became parish priest for Pierrefonds, Marc for Chassors. Their integration into their respective communities was not always easy. Together we had to discover the priest's role in a L'Arche community. This essential role enabled the community to grow and deepen its life and help it to put down roots.

In 1986, Bishop Adolphe-Marie Hardy, the second successor to Bishop Desmazières, accepted the request of another assistant, Philip Kearney, to be ordained as a priest for L'Arche. After three years of preparation, he was ordained on March 11, 1989. Each one of these ordinations has confirmed L'Arche's acceptance by the church.

## *The place of priests in L'Arche*

L'Arche communities are communities of lay people. What, then, is a priest's role?

In Fr. Thomas, we had the model of a hidden, contemplative priest. Little by little we discovered another, more active model. Some priests are members of their community councils and participate in working out the community's priorities and fundamental orientations.

Priests in L'Arche are to be constant reminders of the spiritual dimension of our lives that is so vital to our community life; they remind us that we all need to be nourished regularly by God's word and the eucharist. There is always the risk of falling back into the values of security, wealth, comfort and power. Without this spiritual dimension and growth in holiness, L'Arche could become simply another group home. It would lose what makes it unique. It can be difficult, however, to find priests or men and women of God who understand L'Arche.

The unity between the priest and the director is vital for the life of each community. Over the years, there has been tension and joy. Sometimes directors do not want the priest to have any authority. It is easier for directors to call on different priests for help, without giving any real authority to any one of them. In this way, the director keeps all the power for him- or herself.

Priests also have their deficiencies. It is difficult to be in a rather hidden, priestly role, at the service of the spiritual growth of individual members and of the community as a whole. It can be difficult for priests to see the deficiencies of the community without judging or condemning it. Priests can find it difficult to be accountable to the community for what they do, to be evaluated and called to grow in certain areas; it is easier just to take advantage of the community as a good place to be, a source of nourishment for themselves.

In the history of L'Arche, the relationship between priests and directors has been full of tensions—but these tensions can be healthy. They come from differences in temperament and the necessity to readjust and define the limits of responsibility. We all need to learn how to live and grow through these tensions. Too often in the history of the church, there has been a radical split between temporal and spiritual authority in order to eliminate tension. This radical split is just as wrong as it is confusing. Community leaders also have a responsibility on the spiritual level. They are called to be good shepherds, to care for and nourish their people. They are not simply good administrators. In the same way, priests are called to play a role in temporal affairs. However, the split and rivalry between the two can exist in a L'Arche community when one authority tries to exclude the other. The only solution is communion between the two and the recognition that each one has a gift to exercise for the good of the whole body which is the community.

A priest is not there just as a friend whom the community leader has chosen. He must have a certain independence vis-à-vis the leader. He has received a mission from Jesus and from the church; he is sent to the community. At times he must be free to denounce evil and injustice. But above all he is called to be a gentle and humble shepherd, serving the community and its individual members. He knows their limits and weaknesses, but he is there to affirm them, to walk with them patiently and kindly, sustaining them gently rather than pushing them too hard. His model is Jesus, who washes the feet of his disciples.

A meeting of priests from L'Arche communities and the International Council was held in Rome in January 1984. Thirty-seven priests attended from twenty-eight communities. At this meeting the distinction between priests *of* L'Arche and priests *for* L'Arche became clearer. Priests *of* L'Arche are those whose main ministry is in a L'Arche community. Priests *for* L'Arche exercise a ministry in L'Arche in a limited way for a limited time. Priests *of* L'Arche are called to help other priests in the region find their place in their communities. They are also present at events L'Arche organizes: meetings, Covenant retreats, Renewals, retreats for people with handicaps, Commissions, etc. We are seeing more and more clearly that the role of priests in the growth and development of the spiritual and mystical life of community members is to help them put down roots in community life.

The priests in L'Arche feel a need to meet, share and pray together—to form a real fraternity. They are reflecting on a "Fraternity of priests in L'Arche," for which Fr. Thomas had been asked to write a draft charter.

## Accompanying bishops

In many countries where L'Arche has taken root, an accompanying bishop links our communities with the national conference of bishops. In France, Bishop Adolphe-Marie Hardy, Bishop of Beauvais, invites the priests accompanying our communities to meet together once a year. Bishop Paul Lanneaux, Auxiliary Bishop of Brussels, does the same for our priests in Belgium. In England, Bishop John Rawsthorne, Roman Catholic Auxiliary Bishop of Liverpool, works closely with Bishop Martin Wharton, accompanying Bishop of the Church of England, and the Reverend Graham Cook, who represents the Free Church Federal Council. All three meet regularly with the Regional Coordinators and occasionally with priests and ministers who are close to our communities. We hope that there will soon be accompanying bishops for L'Arche in each country. Their presence does not, of course, replace the links each community should have with its local bishop.

## The Pontifical Council for the Laity

In 1981, with covenant retreats, Gilbert and Marc's ordination, the commitment of other priests to L'Arche and L'Arche's expansion—especially in Third World countries, we felt the need to have direct contact with the Roman authorities of the Roman Catholic Church. While on pilgrimage in Rome with a group from Trosly at Christmas of that year, I spoke about this with Fr. Pedro Arrupé, then the Superior General of the Jesuits. He suggested that I meet with

Cardinal Pironio. One day, someone told me that Cardinal Pironio was at the Little Sisters of Jesus, where we were staying. In that very providential way, I met him and talked with him about L'Arche. He was clearly touched and interested by what I told him.

During a Faith and Light meeting in Rome, I met Fr. Peter Coughlan of the Pontifical Council for the Laity. This Pontifical Council had been created to support Roman Catholic lay associations and link them with Rome. Fr. Coughlan became interested in L'Arche, and invited the International Coordinator (who was then Sue Mosteller) and me to visit him. Our first conversations were friendly. We tried to see how we could give L'Arche some status or recognition that would help us deepen and be faithful to the Holy Spirit's initial inspiration. Clearly, the majority of assistants who were putting roots down in L'Arche were not there just for a job; they were motivated by a deep desire to follow Jesus. They received the strength and nourishment they needed in order to live on a permanent basis with people in need through their faith and their sense of belonging to their church.

L'Arche could not be defined as a Roman Catholic association because, from the beginning, our vocation was ecumenical and inter-faith. We are a Federation of communities, each one integrated into its local church or religious tradition. This integration differs according to the community's ecumenical or inter-faith vocation. Still, quite a number of Roman Catholic assistants desire their church's support and recognition.

The dialogue with the Pontifical Council for the Laity was not always easy. When, however, Cardinal Pironio was named President of this Council, his presence and his way of listening to us were helpful. He enabled us to have the Pontifical Council for the Laity accept an accompanying bishop for Roman Catholics in L'Arche. L'Arche chose Archbishop

Peter Sutton, o.m.i., archbishop in Canada's far northern diocese of Keewatin-Le Pas and a long-time friend of L'Arche.

Every year now, the International Coordinator (Sue, Claire, and now Jo), the Vice-Coordinator (when possible), Archbishop Sutton and I meet with the Pontifical Council for the Laity to share with Cardinal Pironio and others. I think that is why I received an invitation to participate in the Synod on the Mission of the Laity that took place in Rome in 1987. Following the synod, the pope's final document mentioned ecumenical associations for the first time in an official document from Rome.

## L'Arche's ecumenical vocation

L'Arche's first seeds were planted in the earth of the Roman Catholic Church. Through God's grace, other seeds were planted in other soils. Steve and Ann Newroth, both from the Anglican Church, founded Canada's first community. Gabrielle Einsle founded Asha Niketan in India, the first inter-faith community. It is good to remember that the inter-denominational and inter-faith aspect of L'Arche was not one of its basic principles. L'Arche became ecumenical when it welcomed men and women with handicaps who belonged to different denominations and different religions. L'Arche wants to help all persons grow and deepen the faith they have received from their families, and be integrated into their specific churches or religious tradition. This means that L'Arche wants to walk humbly with different traditions, not create its own church with its own rules, worship and liturgy. It means we must move slowly with different persons who come from different theological differences and disciplines, especially the ones around inter-communion. It means also that we share their deep thirst for unity and the recognition of all that unites us as followers of Jesus.

79

L'Arche communities in North America and Great Britain began very naively in this domain. Little by little, we discovered all the questions, difficulties, and tensions involved in an ecumenical vocation.

In its desire to help people deepen their life in their own tradition, L'Arche has chosen various ways of celebrating its liturgies and community prayers during international meetings or in interdenominational communities. Each community must have a place of unity. All L'Arche communities have as their basic principle of unity God's presence in the poor, who bring us closer to God. To recognize God's presence in the poor, we need to be men and women of prayer, deeply nourished in our own faith.

Some of our communities are rooted in a single tradition, be it Roman Catholic, Anglican or Protestant. They find support and encouragement from their church, which mandates a priest or minister to accompany the community. They remain open to members who belong to other traditions and need to find their rightful place in the community. Other communities are interdenominational or inter-faith. When a community is not rooted in a particular tradition, questions arise. How can it be helped and nourished as a community of faith? How can it nourish and encourage its members in their faith journey, according to gospel values? Who can mandate priests, ministers or spiritual guides to accompany the community and be responsible for its spiritual growth? That is why we encourage each community to clarify its religious identity and why we need to reflect more carefully on the role of pastoral ministers in an interdenominational community.

L'Arche is gradually discovering its own spirituality and identity, which differ from those of religious orders or communities founded on the same faith and liturgy. L'Arche also differs from group homes, which are not faith communities. This gradual discovery and acceptance of who we are does not come without pain. It would be so much simpler if we all belonged to the same tradition or if our spiritual life could be reduced to each person's private affair. However, L'Arche's challenge is to unify the need to respect each person in his or her faith journey with each person's need to belong to a community of faith.

In Great Britain, it took some time for our communities to find Anglican bishops to accompany them (Bishops Stephen Verney, Richard Third and Graham Chadwick). Together these communities live and celebrate all that is possible in the unity of faith: prayer, the word of God, preparations for the sacraments, pilgrimages, etc.

In June 1994, Jo Lenon, the International Coordinator, and I met with members of the World Council of Churches in Geneva, and in October 1994, we shared with Dr. George Carey, Archbishop of Canterbury.

*Jean Vanier with Archbishop Robert Runcie,*
*Archbishop of Canterbury, during a retreat Jean*
*gave there in September 1983*

To help us reflect more deeply on these questions, the International Council encouraged the election of an ecumenical commission in each Zone. These commissions maintain contact with the Pontifical Council for Promoting Christian Unity in Rome and the ecumenical offices of different churches in various countries.

We do not live these questions alone; other communities are struggling with the gift of ecumenism: Roger Schutz and the Taizé community in France, the Community of Grandchamp in Switzerland, the Church of the Saviour in the United States, and the Focolari communities throughout the world. There is dialogue and contact between the different traditions. Bishops and theologians of various denominations meet, share together and publish documents and working papers. All of this points in the same direction: a desire for dialogue and cooperation for the sake of the kingdom and the recognition that we are all brothers and sisters in Christ. Along with these other communities, L'Arche wants to live this reality in its daily life, with all the incumbent pain and misunderstandings, as well as joys and hopes. L'Arche wants to respond to the thirst for unity in the heart of Jesus.

V

# STRUCTURING L'ARCHE

## (1982-1994)

### The Fifth Federation Meeting
### (South Bend, Indiana, U.S.A., 1982)

The Federation meeting in South Bend in 1982 was, like the one in Chateauneuf, a time of celebration, a meeting place for people coming from L'Arche communities throughout the world. Sixty-three communities were represented, along with observers from new projects. At the meeting, the General Assembly voted on the orientations for a new constitution. With the growing number of communities and regions, and the consequent increase in the number of regional coordinators, the International Council had become too big. We no longer had enough time at Council meetings to address with any depth basic questions that were coming up. So, the Assembly decided to create three Zones (the Americas, Europe-Africa-Middle East, and Asia-West Pacific), each with a Zone Coordinator and a Zone Council. They would bring together the regional coordinators, who would now be responsible for supporting communities and new projects in their regions. The new International Council, which consisted of the International Coordinators, the Zone Coordinators and myself, received the mission to deepen the vision and vocation of the L'Arche communities and establish directions to help them deepen their life, and be faithful to God and their people. We are continually learning how to work together, support one another, and affirm and challenge each other.

The International Council set up these new structures when Sue Mosteller and Hubert Allier (who had replaced Alain Saint Macary as Vice Coordinator in 1982) were the International Coordinators. The structures became a reality at the 1984 International Council meeting at which Claire de Miribel and Joe Egan were named to succeed Sue and Hubert. At that same meeting the Council named zone coordinators: Robert Larouche and Margaret O'Donnell for the Americas, Jacques Macabeo and Katherine Hall for Europe-Africa-Middle East, and Hazel Bradley for Asia-West Pacific.

## Crises and setbacks

Perhaps it would be useful to say a word about some of the crises and setbacks we experienced, especially during the early days of L'Arche. I have already spoken about my naiveté. Maybe that same naiveté exists in every new foundation. Because people have no experience and cannot foresee everything, they must act with trust and leave room for Providence. There can, however, be a lack of wisdom. But it is also true that we learn, hopefully, from crises and failures to see more clearly where God is leading us and how God wants us to act, live and develop.

### Communities that left the Federation

The first community that had to leave was Maryfarm, a small community near Ottawa, Canada. The community leaders, Frank and Anne Marie Collard, were a wonderful, generous couple who, with their children, were deeply anchored in the love of Jesus. When Maryfarm was welcomed into L'Arche in 1974, the community was not aware of all the structures and requirements that belonging to L'Arche involved. When they discovered the structures and various requirements, they decided to leave. This was very painful for them and us.

Maria Huset in Norway and Mount L'Arche in Montana, U.S.A., left L'Arche in 1981 and 1983 respectively. Once again, this was very painful for them and us. All these situations and events helped us see that, before a new community becomes part of L'Arche, it is important for it to get to know L'Arche's life-style, structures and requirements, and to forge bonds with other members of the family. We realized how vital it is, for example, that the founding director and founding team spend several years in an already existing community in order to create these bonds and give birth to a new community, a new member of the family.

## Communities that closed

In 1972 the L'Arche community founded by Tom and Mira (née Ziauddin) Chemlir in Kotagiri, India, was the first to close, after just nine months. Several factors led to the closure. We had not sufficiently prepared this foundation with the national Board of Directors of Asha Niketan in Bangalore. It had all been done too quickly. And finally, Tom and Mira felt that this was not their vocation, and returned to the United States. The community in Bangalore welcomed the people with handicaps who had lived with Tom and Mira.

The community in Man (Ivory Coast) also had to close in 1978. L'Arche Bouaké was founded in 1975. We thought it would be good to open another community close by. Bishop Agré, of Man, strongly encouraged us to come to his diocese, found a property and helped us build a house. However, we realized afterwards that the newly founded community in Bouaké was not strong enough to take on the responsibility of a new foundation. We had to close the house in Man; the community in Bouaké welcomed the people we had received at Man.

In 1981, the community of Emmaus in Milton, Australia, was founded with the help and support of the parish priest, who welcomed L'Arche as a parish project. But when he was transferred to another parish, the new parish priest was not interested in the L'Arche project; that created many difficulties. Because of those difficulties, we had to close the community in 1986. Three of the people we had welcomed there went to the community of Genesaret; the fourth went to an institution that seemed more adapted to her particular needs.

In 1990, l'Ecureuil in Sainte Thècle, Québec, had to close because it was too isolated. For the same reason, the community in Saint Prosper had to move; it joined le Printemps in Saint Malachie. We realize that if a community is to survive, grow and deepen, it has to be in an area that can provide it with friends and support.

*Other setbacks*

A certain number of setbacks were caused by the departures of directors who had not received sufficient support. Consequently, they had great difficulties and left when disaster struck.

This kind of departure was painful for the community and the directors. Had there been more vigilance, support and wisdom, we could have avoided some pain. These painful situations, however, have helped us to see how important it is to establish the length of the appointments for directors— especially founding directors. After the first appointment, we now have a time of evaluation and discernment to see if the person should continue for a second term or allow someone else to take over the responsibility.

This discernment has not eliminated all the pain. It is still difficult for founding directors not to be asked to continue. They then leave with a sense of failure and a wound that can last many years.

Other directors have left their positions of responsibility, but wanted to remain in the community; their presence, however, seemed too threatening for the new directors, so they had to leave. This was especially true if the new director was young, inexperienced and unable to take on full responsibility if the former director remained. This was particularly true if the community was small.

These painful situations and setbacks made the International Council look more closely at the Federation's admission procedures and the way communities are formed. In North America, many communities grew up around one person who knew L'Arche: the founder became the director. But it is difficult to create community and communicate the spirit of L'Arche all alone. We had to clarify how we support new projects; we decided we should not commit ourselves to any project unless, from the beginning, two or three people are committed to it for a good length of time. Two of us, Fr. Thomas and I, founded L'Arche; other friends very quickly came to help. One person alone cannot create community.

*Crises in communities*

The fact that we welcomed assistants who obviously did not have a vocation for L'Arche caused a number of crises in our communities. These people lacked a certain stability and balance. Sometimes they were trying to prove themselves and did not agree with L'Arche's basic orientation. In some cases, there was open conflict, and the assistant had to be dismissed.

Some of these situations were so serious and painful that they even threatened the community's life. Some conflicts and difficulties were resolved only through good support and help from members of the Boards of Directors.

All these crises helped us see more clearly L'Arche's ambiguities: we wanted to be a Christian community, firmly anchored in the values of the gospel; at the same time we wanted to be a facility regulated by state norms. How can these two aspects be reconciled? Our criteria for choosing assistants must be wiser and clearer; we must learn how to discern better if they are truly called to L'Arche, and set up a system of practical formation and evaluation.

## *Crises with the government and neighbours*

I already mentioned that, because of lack of dialogue, the people in Trosly took up a petition against L'Arche in 1971. Other crises arose when neighbours opposed the creation of a L'Arche community in their area. Perhaps the most important of these was in Kansas City in the United States.

In 1984, Christella Buser and her Board were ready to buy a house and begin a new community. They had chosen the neighbourhood and explained their project to some of neighbours. But when they presented it to the Municipal Council it was rejected: other neighbours had protested; they did not want people with mental handicaps in their neighbourhood. And they won! The Board and the neighbours went through the same scenario three more times. Then Christella organized a whole network of friends who sent letters and telegrams to the Municipal Council; she and Board members made personal visits to senators. Finally, in 1988, they were able to change the zoning laws and buy a duplex in Overland Park, Kansas. We are still very far from being a world that welcomes people with handicaps.

In France the Ministry of Social Security reacted strongly to our policy of not paying assistants normal salaries. No French laws allow centres to have volunteers or assistants with lower salaries. It took us several years to negotiate this question with government officials and with the Social Security. For us, the issue was quite clear: young assistants coming to L'Arche to live an ideal of community life did not need regular salaries; they were coming to live something that could not be measured in financial terms. They receive a stipend and, of course, room and board. This allows them to deepen and clarify their motivations.

To help government authorities understand and accept our vision, we had to dialogue with them. In 1981, we helped the Ministry of Social Affairs grasp what was at stake for L'Arche. We reached an agreement with the Ministry of Labour and the Social Security: during the first two years, assistants at L'Arche are considered to be in formation; they receive a stipend and social security benefits. After two years, they will receive the minimum wage. Obviously L'Arche's system differs from others; community life is very demanding.

I am amazed, however, by the number of men and women in the social services who understand the real needs of people with handicaps and who appreciate L'Arche's values.

Perhaps it was Mademoiselle Berger, when she was the head of the Department of Social Welfare in Beauvais, who understood and explained most clearly the position, questions and concerns that people in authority had with regard to L'Arche. When I met with her in 1977 to explain what L'Arche was, she said to me, "I admire what you are doing. It is surely the best thing for people with handicaps. But if something goes wrong—for example, if assistants accepting small salaries and your lifestyle of life no longer come—what can I do to help you? If I give you subsidies, what guarantee do I have that L'Arche will be able to continue?" She was pointing out the folly of L'Arche. People with mental handicaps need to belong to a place that gives them security. That security of love and belonging is the foundation of growth. But what guarantee do we have that assistants who want to become their friends, share their lives, and create community with them will continue to come? It has become clearer and clearer that L'Arche must learn how to dialogue and work with government authorities; they need to understand L'Arche more deeply so they can support our options by modifying certain laws if necessary, or permitting exceptions.

## The Sixth Federation Meeting (Rome, 1987)

The Federation meeting in Rome, which brought together 350 people from eighty-two communities, was like the two preceding international meetings: a time of celebration, thanksgiving and prayer. As the years go by, we realize more and more how much we are one family and how deeply God has united us. All of us have suffered over the years. All of us are called to celebrate together. The visit of Mother Teresa and a meeting with Pope John-Paul II marked this meeting.

The General Assembly adopted the new constitution, which created three Zones. Two years later, in February 1989, the International Council saw that it was necessary to increase the number of Zones to support the Regions better, and through them, the individual communities. The Regional Coordinators for all the Zones had met in Boston in November 1988 and worked on this plan; at the same meeting the General Assembly gave Claire and Joe a second mandate as International Coordinators.

## The foundation of new communities

New L'Arche communities continued to be born, but with more wisdom and prudence. The Regional Council and the Zone Council followed each new project more closely. The Directors received a very clear mandate, and we helped board members enter into a deeper understanding of L'Arche.

There are two kinds of foundations: foundations that are born from already existing L'Arche communities or Regions, and foundations that are born from outside groups that ask to join the Federation. So it was that the Central American and Caribbean Region gave birth to new communities in Mexico, Choluteca (Honduras), Sao Paulo (Brazil) and Santo Domingo (Dominican Republic). In Europe, on the other hand, the new communities in Germany, Italy, Switzerland and Spain were encouraged and often created by people or groups who knew L'Arche but were outside of it; they became part of L'Arche after much work and time with a coordinator and an accompaniment team. The birth of a new community, in either case, happens over a prolonged period of time.

I would like to say a few words here about two communities created by L'Arche outside of any existing Region: Beit-al Rafiq in Bethany (West Bank) and Punla in Manila (Philippines).

Beit-al Rafiq was born of a call in the heart of Fr. Peter de Brul, a Jesuit professor at the University of Bethlehem. In October 1986, after ten years of preparation and discernment, we welcomed Rula and Armad. The first L'Arche community in an Arab culture was born. However, during the Gulf War, it had to close. Hopefully we will be able to reopen it with more involvement of Palestinian people.

Punla, "little seed," was founded in Manila by Jing Amparo, a Filipino who had spent two years in L'Arche-Liverpool, then six months in Asha Niketan, Madras. He then went back to Manila and worked for two years in an institution for people with mental handicaps. He returned to Madras for another six months and then went to Trosly for six months at La Semence, to gain more experience in a home for people with severe handicaps. Finally in 1988, after all this experience in L'Arche, he welcomed the first two children, Ray and Cere, into the community.

In 1992, three communities in three new countries became part of the Federation.

A community was born in Hungary, near Budapest, founded by Ildiko Draskoczy from Hungary. I had met her a few years before in East Germany where I had been invited to give a talk on L'Arche at a Lutheran Church conference. Ildiko eventually came to live in L'Arche-Trosly and then in

Lambeth-L'Arche. After a time of discernment, she felt called to begin La Barka in her home country.

In 1992, Kana-no-ie, an already existing community in Japan, became a probationary member of L'Arche. It had been founded in 1982, when Sato and his wife, Fumie, welcomed into their own home a few men from an institution. When they heard about L'Arche, they asked to become part of the Federation. It took a few years to reflect with them and to work on their community structures before we celebrated their acceptance into L'Arche in January 1992.

Anne Kiruta, a Ugandan, opened a community in Kampala, Uganda. Her five years in Lambeth-L'Arche had prepared her well for this foundation. Like our other communities in West Africa, L'Arche-Kampala welcomes children. However, it is the first community on the African continent whose founding director comes from the same country.

Now, in 1995, new projects are developing with people in Zimbabwe, Holland and Syria.

What is striking is that even with all the preparations and attention these new foundations have received, and in spite of the help the Boards have given, many new communities go through difficult moments, unexpected crises and tensions. It is as if each new community has to make the passage in faith from the community as "my project" or "our project" to the community as "God's work."

## A cornerstone for L'Arche

On February 4th, 1993, Fr. Thomas died at the age of 87. He had spent the last two years of his life in Rimont with his brother, Fr. Marie-Dominique Philippe. Tired and aging, he could no longer face the number of people in difficulty who wanted to see him; he had to leave La Ferme. This separation was painful for him as well as for the community. During those two years of absence, he continued to offer his life and

*Jean and Dominican Father Thomas Philippe*

suffering for L'Arche and for all those he had known, supported and accompanied over the years.

His funeral mass was celebrated in Trosly. He was buried in the community, next to the chapel of la Ferme where he had faithfully celebrated the daily eucharist for over twenty years.

The presence of his body, buried at the heart of L'Arche like a cornerstone, is very significant for us all. Fr. Thomas had called me to live with people with mental handicaps in L'Arche. He had discovered their value and importance for society and the church. We miss his warmth and compassion. L'Arche remains attached to his vision and spirituality which continue to inspire us.

His death followed the death of my mother, Pauline "Mamie" Vanier, in 1991, at the age of 93. Their absence leaves an emptiness in Trosly; we miss their compassion and ever-welcoming presence.

## The Seventh Federation Meeting
## (Cap Rouge, Canada, 1993)

Five hundred people from one hundred communities participated in the seventh Federation meeting in 1993. The very fact that we were all together, deeply united despite the fact that we came from such different communities and cultures, gave us a greater awareness of the gift of L'Arche. In spite of our diversity, we truly belong to one family; we are one in heart and one in spirit. The ninety-nine percent of the three hundred voting participants who voted in favour of the new Charter expressed this unity.

### The new Charter

The first Charter of L'Arche, written in 1970 at the foundation of Asha Niketan in Bangalore, described the main objectives of our communities in an inter-faith context. In 1973, after the first Federation meeting, a specifically Christian Charter was written for the Christian communities of

L'Arche. Many found it difficult to accept that we had two different charters; this meant that still others might be written. Shouldn't we, as an international family, be able to agree on a single Charter? The International Council worked on unifying the two Charters. During the whole process, there was consultation with each community. The delegates to the 1993 Federation meeting voted on the final text. With all our diversity, the unity of the essential vision of L'Arche expressed in the new Charter was a sign that God's Spirit was present among us, continuing to gently guide us.

## A new Constitution

The same majority also voted to accept a new International Constitution at that same Federation meeting. The new constitution increased the number of international coordinators and affirmed that the responsibility for L'Arche rests on four "pillars": community leaders with community councils, boards of directors, pastoral ministers and long-term assistants. We hope to involve these four pillars in the responsibility and decision-making of L'Arche at all different levels: in individual communities, regions, zones, and in the International Council.

## New international leaders

In 1993, Claire de Miribel and Joe Egan had completed their second term as International Coordinator and Vice-Coordinator. Therefore, they were no longer eligible for another term. According to our constitution, new international coordinators are voted in by the International Council and the Regional Coordinators on proposals from a discernment team. So, before the 1993 Federation meeting, the International Council had named the discernment team, which consulted with all the communities. In May 1993, Jo Lenon succeeded Claire as International Coordinator. Three Vice Coordinators were elected: Émile Marolleau (second term), Robert Larouche and Alain Saint Macary.

# VI

# QUESTIONS FACING L'ARCHE IN 1995

Today L'Arche is at a turning point. There are more than one hundred communities and twelve new projects. Although many assistants have put down their roots in L'Arche, there is still a great shortage of assistants. Our communities are still quite fragile. In many countries people with handicaps live in difficult situations and are waiting for a home. At each new stage of our history, there are new questions, new challenges. Let me tell you briefly about some of our questions today.

## The unity of the L'Arche family

*Maintaining unity*

Since 1964, L'Arche has grown. How can we keep our communities united, one in heart, one in spirit? We are so different: different cultures, languages, religions. We live in poor countries as well as rich ones. Our unity is rooted in the presence at the heart of each of our communities of the weak and powerless, who call us to compassion and celebration. They are a source of life and of difficulties, too. Living as a family, however, also means finding ways to communicate and come together.

When L'Arche was younger, each community was small and fragile; each one needed the others' friendship and support. Communities living in the same region gathered together frequently; this gave them strength to carry on. Today, our communities have developed their own work programs and have more community meetings; this leaves them less open and less available for gatherings with the larger family. There is a danger that each community will become too self-sufficient, and count only on its own strength. When L'Arche was smaller, people knew each other. Even though they were in different communities, their mutual love brought them close together to support each other. Now there are fewer of these natural bonds of friendship.

New generations have come through L'Arche and the number of assistants has grown. An organization like ours could quickly come to resemble a multi-national with the necessary structures and finances for running our houses, and lose the quality of relationship and friendship. Because they are no longer in the same Zone, communities in France, for example, could easily ignore the gifts and beauty of our communities in the United Kingdom, Germany, Ireland, Belgium and Poland, even though great distances do not separate them.

Perhaps one of our greatest challenges for the future will be maintaining the links of friendship, love and appreciation between the members of the larger family of L'Arche. We will need to keep the lines of communication open and find ways to share with other communities beyond the boundaries of countries, cultures or continents. It is in part a question of organization: renewals, retreats, meetings and formation programs on the international level are important. However, each one of us is responsible for cultivating and nourishing the bonds of friendship between communities.

*Support in times of crisis*

Crises are a natural part of life. They are important times of growth as well as cries for help. We need to be very attentive to a community's life. It is not easy to remain faithful, fully alive, loving, welcoming, accepting of differences. Fatigue, stress and difficulties of all sorts encourage us to seek what is secure, easier and more comfortable. There will always be a lack of assistants. How can we help communities remain open and faithful to Providence, so they do not close in on themselves? When difficulties arise, how can we help assistants to continue to trust in their call to live with people with mental handicaps? Hopefully our structures will continue to support, nourish and help communities walk through crises and remain alive, open and patient during times of trial and tribulation.

Our communities are counter-cultural. In many countries today excellent things are being done for people with handicaps. However, to live with people who are powerless, to become their friends, is still considered by most people, even many people in the churches, as something crazy. The gospel is truly "good news" for the poor, but it appears to be "bad news" for those who are rich in culture, aptitudes and possible life choices. God calls people in such quiet, discrete ways to follow the path of the beatitudes and enter into a spirit of poverty in order to live the fullness of love and inner peace.

*Towards new structures*

Structures are necessary to give support and maintain unity. They constantly need to be adapted to L'Arche's needs as it evolves and develops. That is why a new International Constitution was adopted at the last Federation meeting. It affirms the role of the four "pillars" at all the different levels of L'Arche. These four pillars—community leaders, boards of directors, pastoral ministers and long-term assistants—are called, according to their different functions, to be partners in supporting L'Arche. We hope to implement this principle more fully in the years to come, particularly in the zones and on the international level.

## Solidarity and finances

The needs of each of our communities are so great that sometimes they prevent us from living in solidarity with other communities. Some of our communities receive no government funding; others receive very little, and still others receive substantial grants. Are we not all called to live in solidarity with men and women throughout the world? Have our richer countries discovered all that countries in Africa, India and Latin America have to offer: their sense of humanity, welcome and family? Each country, culture and community has a gift to share with the others and should never be closed in on itself. It is important to continue to share money, assistants, and friendship, so that we are truly a family beyond the boundaries of country, race or religion—a family of the poor.

This sense of solidarity means that we have to seek funds creatively and be open to the signs of Providence. L'Arche began during a time of world economic expansion that enabled us to find the necessary finances for our communities. Today this economic expansion is over. Yet the number of communities has grown; our support system and accompaniment of individual members and communities cost more because they have developed. Where will we find the necessary funding? What principles will guide us? L'Arche International has been functioning since 1969 on gifts and legacies, a sign that Providence has been watching over us in a special way. How do we move into the future with our ever-growing needs? All of us together must carry the financial responsibility for each community as well as for the wider L'Arche family. Each community needs to find men and women who can help us to be wise and competent in this area. Money is an ambiguous reality. We must learn how to find it and how to use it wisely.

## Spirituality and anthropology

### Spreading L'Arche's spirituality

The values of efficiency, power, money and pleasure have become all-important in our world today. They tend to eliminate the values of compassion, humility and presence to the powerless. The mass media nourish and encourage this vision rooted in force, in which exteriority and appearance are more important than interiority and being. We constantly need people to remind us of where true inner freedom and peace are to be found. Each person and each community needs to find spiritual guides who can help keep the flame of love burning. L'Arche has a specific spirituality. It is rooted in the folly of the gospels. It is something quite small, like a seed. It is a "little way," the way of poverty and simplicity. The presence of pastoral ministers, men and women of prayer, is a vital reminder of what is essential for our community life.

If God's word does not nourish our hearts, then we may easily turn into an institution. Community life, which involves sharing, compassion and caring for one another, can disappear and we will simply function as a group home. Our Charter states that we are called to be competent, but this competence must be inspired and imbued by love for each person, and rooted in a life of prayer.

### A vision of the human person

As we welcome people who are weak and powerless and try to give them their rightful place in community, we are discovering a vision of the human person that is very close to the gospel's. Over these last years, we have taken time to reflect on and deepen L'Arche's spirituality. Now, with the help of competent men and women from various fields of the human sciences, we want to reflect on our vision of the human person. We need to rediscover the laws of human growth and development. It would be dangerous to deepen a spirituality that did not have a good anthropological basis.

We have a treasure in L'Arche. People with mental handicaps reveal important elements of our human nature that are often hidden in people who have developed their intellectual and manual capacities. We will have to deepen, explain and reflect on these elements to show what it means to grow and develop as a human being, and what we need in order to live and deepen our humanity.

*Celibacy and long-term commitments*

We need to find ways to give better support to assistants who are called to follow Jesus by living the gift of celibacy for the kingdom (cf. Matthew 19:22). How do we affirm it clearly as a vocation in L'Arche and in the church? In the 1986 meeting in Australia, the International Council named two commissions to reflect on the question of celibacy and to propose clearer directions to assistants who sense such a call. These commissions organized meetings and made proposals to the International Council.

We also shared during the two Covenant Journeys that were held in Europe in October 1988 and in the Americas in January 1989. About 120 assistants participated in these "Journeys"; each had lived at least five years in L'Arche and had affirmed the Covenant twice. For ten days we met in a climate of prayer to share our journey in faith and speak of what we needed to deepen our specific vocation and our roots in L'Arche.

This question of celibacy is an important one in L'Arche today. The quality of our communities depends on the quality of life in our homes, which in turn depends on the commitment of assistants who put down roots in the life of the home. Long-term assistants living in a house can help younger assistants grow in and deepen their relationship with those who have handicaps, and eventually put down roots. If few long-term assistants live in a house, then the homes function with assistants who are there for a short period. The people with handicaps suffer the most from this.

If God has called L'Arche into existence, it is to reveal himself to the poor. This revelation involves the presence of single, committed, long-term assistants, assistants for whom L'Arche is truly a call, a vocation. Communities must do everything they can to make this vocation possible; to make sure that these assistants are accompanied and nourished; that they have a rhythm of life that allows them to live the long haul. It also means that communities must establish clear criteria for welcoming new assistants and discerning those who are called to this way of life. This is one of our challenges for the coming years.

## Families

More and more families are committed to L'Arche. Some, like Pat and Jo Lenon, came as a family and are committed to a community. Others, like Denis and Lynn Blin, Jean and Anne-Marie de la Selle, first came and lived in L'Arche as single assistants, then married and continued to live in L'Arche after their marriage. In L'Arche-Trosly there are presently about forty families, with a number of children. The presence of families is a real treasure. In the March 1987 issue of the *Letters of L'Arche,* Joe Egan wrote lengthily about this. There are questions, however: how do we help families participate fully in the community's life and see the community as a place that nourishes each person and welcome his or her gifts, and not just a workplace for one of the partners? Of course, it is the same for single assistants.

Sometimes there is so much to do in our communities that assistants can miss the essential reason for their presence: belonging, communion and growth in love. This issue comes up in all communities, not only in L'Arche. We can so easily replace the quality of relationships by rules, regulations, and things to do.

## Challenges to L'Arche's identity

*Communities that honour difference*

Our communities are disconcerting. They bring together people who are so different. First of all, we welcome people whose handicaps are very different. Assistants, too, are very diverse: some are married (and here again, no two families are alike); some are single, committed to celibacy; others are undecided about it. We are far from being homogeneous communities where everyone adheres to the same expression of faith in the same way. Each person has very different needs.

All of us tend to want a strong homogeneous community that gives security. We can forget that priority is given to each individual person and to his or her needs for personal growth. L'Arche communities have a real weakness because of the great diversity of their members, their vocations and ways of expressing their faith. This weakness calls us to greater respect and love for each person in his or her specific call and gifts; it also means we have to clarify and emphasize those realities which are sources of unity: the heart of God and the hearts of those who are the poorest and the weakest; communion with God and communion with the poorest and the weakest. Our communities are built on these two poles. If we do not build on them, then the communities will gradually die or be transformed into institutions. Therefore, each member of a community must be nourished to grow in love, inner healing, freedom and holiness.

*Faith communities* and *professional centres for people with handicaps*

Faith communities *and* professional centres for people with handicaps: this reveals the deepest ambiguity of our communities. They must be competent and well administered, because we are responsible for the people who have been entrusted to us. We need the right medical and psychological support to help them grow towards greater autonomy and wholeness. At the same time, L'Arche wants to be a faith community. For that reason L'Arche needs priests, ministers and spiritual guides who remind us of our fundamental vocation. The history of communities shows that after the first period of foundation, which is a time of spiritual enthusiasm and trust in poverty, a period of search for security, wealth and comfort follows. During this time laws and regulations risk replacing the spirit of love, risk and trust in God. Will L'Arche know how to avoid this movement towards institutionalization? In many countries today, government authorities recognize, value and appreciate L'Arche; we receive government subsidies and government grants. Will we be able to keep our hearts open? Will we still be able to take risks in the future? Will we know how to remain prophetic?

Yes—if we remain faithful in three areas:
(a)  We must remain close and attentive to people with handicaps. If this fundamental communion and friendship no longer exists, then we risk becoming only good managers seeking the security of rules, regulations and good educational principles. Our communion with the poorest will show us the path to follow and keep us true to our vocation. The day that we no longer allow ourselves to be disturbed by love, or that we oblige people to fit into the rigid mould of laws, we are in danger. The day our communities are no longer places of communion, celebration and prayer, but only workplaces and training centres, we are in danger. If we forget that God loves the weakest, most intellectually disabled person who has a privileged place in God's heart, and that his or her fundamental vocation lies in this communion with God, we are in danger.

(b) We must remain true communities, living simply, sharing personally and discerning together. There is always the danger of wanting the security of hierarchy, in which salaries are linked to roles. In community life, responsibility is a service that we are called to assume for a limited period of time. Once this service is completed, we can be asked to take on another role in the community. Salaries are just one example. There are many other consequences to our option for community. For example, a community, with its Board of Directors, needs to commit itself to those assistants who have lived and worked for a long time in the community without much salary. This commitment has financial and administrative consequences.

(c) We must continually deepen our spiritual life. This is a priority. The spiritual life is not just going to church or praying. It is a way of life, the quality of love that should permeate all our gestures and relationships. Our spiritual life allows us to live each moment in communion with God and with our brothers and sisters. "As the Father has loved me, so I have loved you . . .This is my commandment: that you love one another as I have loved you" (John 15: 9-12).

The spirituality of L'Arche has two poles: communion with the Father through prayer, and communion with the poor person who reveals to us God's hidden presence. "Whoever welcomes this child in my name welcomes me, and whoever welcomes me welcomes the one who sent me; for the least among all of you is the greatest" (Luke 9: 48). It is a spirituality of simplicity, humility and trust. It invites us to go *down* the social ladder of success to live in communities of faith in communion with those who are poor.

To live and to deepen L'Arche's spirituality, we need to be linked to the Roman Catholic Church, the "earth" in which L'Arche was born, and to the other Christian churches and religions in which L'Arche has been planted. Each person, each community in L'Arche, needs to drink from the spring flowing in their own faith and tradition. They need to find support and nourishment in God's word, and in the writings and lives of the prophets and saints of each tradition. We must not set these differences up against each other, but try to find what unites us more deeply in our common love for God and those who are weak. We are constantly discovering that one of L'Arche's missions is to spread this spirituality of God's hidden presence in the heart of the weakest. In 1989, the International Council created an international spirituality commission that provides a place where we can study these questions in depth and help each community to be faithful to its vocation.

If our communities try to be faithful in these three areas, God will be with them. God's Spirit will call forth assistants with a vocation for L'Arche, guide us and give us the necessary strength and wisdom.

## L'Arche's identity in different cultures

L'Arche began in Europe. Five years later it was founded in two other cultures: North America and India. Quite soon after that it appeared in Africa, the Caribbean, Latin America, Australia, Japan, and the Philippines. Today there are communities in Eastern Europe and the Middle East. In poorer countries, the first communities were founded by assistants from richer countries, who had discovered L'Arche in Europe or in North America. They, of course, did find good support from local people who accepted them and opened up to them. They embraced the country's culture, but the fact still remained that they were foreigners—and were seen as such, despite their commitment. In these last few years people from the country who had spent time in an already existing community elsewhere founded our new communities. That was the case for Brazil, Uganda and the Philippines, as well as for our new projects in Syria and Zimbabwe. In communities established by foreigners, leaders from the local community have gradually replaced the founders who still remain part of the community. Each L'Arche community is becoming more and more rooted in its country and in its people.

In L'Arche the poor introduce us to their culture, the culture of the poor, which is universal and goes beyond the local culture. Our communities are called to belong to these two cultures: the culture of the country and the culture of the poor. We have to discover and deepen each country's specific way of living L'Arche. Today our communities are trying to formulate the specific challenges to and the identity of L'Arche in their countries and cultures.

In September 1992, our four Asha Niketans met. For one week, community leaders, long-term assistants, board members and spiritual guides worked with professionals and people committed to other types of communities in India. They reviewed L'Arche's history in India, evaluated our community life and our fundamental options, and examined how L'Arche is taking root in the Indian culture. The week bore much fruit and brought real renewal to our communities.

That same year, the communities in North America started a Mission-Identity process which is still going on today. It has already helped L'Arche communities in North America recognize themselves as Christian communities founded on faith in the good news of Jesus.

A similar meeting will take place in 1995 for our seven communities in the Latin America/Caribbean Zone. The meeting, called "Nueva Esperanza" has been well prepared by consultation with all community members, some of whom have been there from the beginning.

# CONCLUSION

When we look back at the history of L'Arche, it is beautiful as well as painful. It is painful because of all the crises and conflicts in our communities, the fatigue and the stress, the people who were sent back to psychiatric hospitals, assistants who sometimes left in anger or disillusionment, and whose leaving hurt many of us, especially those with mental handicaps. When you are vulnerable, thirsting for friendship and communion, it is hard to see people with whom you have begun a relationship of trust leave.

But L'Arche's history is also very beautiful. It is the story of men and women who came to us from asylums, psychiatric hospitals and other situations of rejection and total abandonment, and who have made the passage from death to resurrection, from anguish to trust, from loneliness to community, from despair to hope. They have discovered the good news of Jesus, the good news of God. They were able to make this passage because many wonderful assistants were with them.

It is also the story of many assistants and friends who have found new life and discovered the gospel through their covenant with wounded, weak people; assistants who met and became friends with our people, and then chose to follow Jesus on the path of peace, the path of the beatitudes.

Sometimes all the difficulties we encounter in our communities surprise us; we think that life must be easier in other communities. Unfortunately, this is all part of our human condition. It is important to remember that L'Arche is founded on pain. We are called to welcome men and women who know the pain of being handicapped, but who suffer even more from the pain of rejection and alienation that their handicaps have provoked. Very few are going to be healed and then leave. Our role is to be with them, to walk with them, in their pain and anguish, until the end of their lives. Once they discover that they are loved, that they have a place in a family, a community—once they have discovered the good news of Jesus, they do live a real resurrection. That does not eliminate, however, all the accumulated pain and frustrations of the past years. Our communities are, and always will be, a sign of contradiction, a place where joy and pain, crises and peace are closely interwoven. Our history is both beautiful and painful. It is a history of success and of setbacks. It is a history where cross and resurrection, sin and grace, fear and trust are intimately linked.

Men and women with handicaps have been with us for ten, fifteen and twenty years in some of our communities. They are more peaceful, even happy. Some work and are proud of it. They have acquired certain skills and maturity; they know what they want; their choices are clear. They want to live in L'Arche and welcome others into the community. They want to live with assistants who will be there on a permanent basis. They feel called to live the good news of Jesus. On the other hand, new assistants, who do not always know what they want, join us; they are still trying to find their path in life. There is an ever-widening gap between the maturity of the men and women with handicaps and the immaturity of many new assistants.

Our communities also suffer from a shortage of and a constant change in assistants. This only accentuates the fact that it is the men and women with mental handicaps who are really at home in our communities; L'Arche is truly their home, their family. They are at the heart of L'Arche. But to live their vocation in L'Arche fully, they need assistants who are with them on a long-term basis.

Now that some of our people feel at peace and at home in L'Arche, their deepest vocation is developing. We know that many of them are capable of a certain autonomy, of accomplishing certain tasks and taking on some responsibility. However, they have a deeper capacity: an openness to God, a way of receiving God's gift and entering into an intimate relationship with him. The words of St. Paul are constantly being manifested in our communities: "But God chose what is foolish in the world to shame the wise; God chose what is weak in the world to shame the strong; God chose what is low and despised in the world, things that are not, to reduce to nothing things that are" (1 Corinthians 1:27).

People with mental handicaps are called to holiness. Sometimes we forget that, just as we forget that they are called to become our teachers on the spiritual level. They open up for us a simple path of love. They lead us towards deeper spiritual confidence. They remind us that if we do not become like little children, we will not enter into the kingdom of heaven. There is, however, a great diversity among people with mental handicaps: not all of them have developed a deep spiritual sensitivity; they do not all live an intimate communion with God; each one has his or her own particular struggles and temptations. Each one is on a path. Over the years, however, many of our people have lived through times of great crises.

We realize that many of them have been living the good news of Jesus in a very simple way. We realize that the gospel parable of the wedding feast is being lived out in L'Arche. In the parable, the king is wounded and hurt because many worthy people, well integrated into society, have refused the invitation to the wedding feast. So he sends his servants out to the highways and by-ways, to all the poor, the lame and the blind, to invite them to the wedding feast. And they, of course, come running! Are not those we welcome in L'Arche like the poor in this parable who answer God's invitation and come running to the feast of love?

I am deeply moved as I look over these past thirty years. The beginnings of L'Arche were so poor: Fr. Thomas and I lived a profound unity; a few of us lived in a little house. The seed fell into the earth, grew and bore much fruit. It is the seed of the Holy Spirit who guides everything with wisdom and love. These thirty years have revealed what was contained in that initial seed. Each person with a mental handicap has a message to bring to the church and to the world. He or she is essentially a heart that loves, a heart that calls us to communion and to community. In this way people with mental handicaps are prophetic and, like all prophets, they disturb. They call us to change and to let ourselves be transformed; they invite us to becomes more deeply human, more loving; they invite us to enter into communion and community, instead of throwing ourselves into work, hyperactivity, and seeking success, wealth and reputation. These prophets can be silent: they do not always make much noise. It is easy to ignore them, to put them aside and say that they are useless or even to condemn them to death.

At the same time we need to seek out the truth constantly. Our communities must not live simply on the emotional level; we should not close ourselves off from others. L'Arche needs to listen to what the social sciences have to say about human growth. It also needs to learn from theology, which, rooted in the word of God and the inspiration of the Holy Spirit, calls all people over the centuries to conversion and to discover the way of humility and love.

L'Arche is a place where the good news is announced to the poor and by the poor. These past thirty years and our one hundred and two L'Arche communities, plus the Faith and Light communities, witness to the mysterious power in the

*Hector and Brenda at L'Arche-Suyapa*
*(Tegucigalpa Honduras)*

heart of those who are weak. They have transformed my life and the lives of many others. God seems to use them to awaken our hearts, to lead us to greater wholeness and to give us back our humanity. Jesus used Raphaël, Philippe and many others to form and shape my heart and lead me into greater communion with the Father.

Many assistants who have lived this communion and this covenant with the poor have discovered the mystery of God hidden in weakness, even in their own weakness. This discovery has transformed their hearts and been at the source of many vocations inside, as well as outside of, L'Arche. Besides the number of assistants who have affirmed their covenant with the poor in L'Arche, about one hundred assistants have left Trosly to become priests or to enter religious orders. Still others discovered their vocation to marriage here, and the mystery of Jesus' presence hidden in the littleness of their own children. L'Arche is discerning more and more clearly its vocation to serve the whole church and society.

When I first began L'Arche, I never would have said as clearly as I say today that people with mental handicaps are prophetic. We discovered this gradually over the years, as we searched for our way, our structures and our identity. People with mental handicaps have helped me discover what community is. They are at the origin of the book *Community and Growth* (London: Darton, Longman and Todd, revised edition, 1989). Our society has difficulty understanding community structures. It is much better geared to structures of trade unions in which salaries are given according to specific jobs, years of experience, and acquired privileges. Yet I am convinced that many organizations are looking for structures that allow more sharing, truthfulness and communion which, in turn, give better results and more fruitful work. Many people no longer want to live and work in a world of competition and struggle with its unjust system of salaries. The poor help us rediscover community. In the same way, the poor who show us the path to unity, unity between rich and poor, between Christians of different denominations, people of different religions, between cultures. Their littleness and our common humanity draw us to them and show us a path that leads to peace.

We are celebrating our thirtieth anniversary. We have structures in L'Arche that have proven adequate. My wish is that we continue to be prophetic, that people with mental handicaps—whether they be in L'Arche or outside, waiting for a place of welcome—continually disturb and challenge us. I pray that they may continually call us to deeper faith, greater courage, wisdom and truth. I pray that we will not close ourselves up in what we have learned over these thirty years or in a search for greater security. If we are to remain prophetic, we must remain weak and little. We still have much to receive, learn and discover. We need to constantly allow God's strength and wisdom to manifest themselves through our weakness, so that the weak, the rejected, the so-called foolish, may continue to shame the powerful and the prudent, and show us the path to Love.

L'Arche is not a solution to all problems, but a sign. L'Arche is a sign that love is possible, that the weak, whatever their weakness, have gifts and a message to give. L'Arche is a sign that faith and competence can embrace and work together for the human and spiritual growth and development of each person. It is a sign that institutions can become communities when people work together in a spirit of love and unity. If these thirty years of L'Arche mark the end of the beginning, they are more than anything the beginning of a new stage of growth in depth and influence in society.

# Appendix 1

## Charter of the communities of L'Arche

L'Arche began in 1964 when Jean Vanier and Father Thomas Philippe, in response to a call from God, invited Raphaël Simi and Philippe Seux, two men with mental handicaps, to come and share their life in the spirit of the Gospel and of the Beatitudes that Jesus preached.

From this first community, born in France and in the Roman Catholic tradition, many other communities have developed in various cultural and religious traditions.

These communities, called into being by God, are united by the same vision and the same spirit of welcome, of sharing and simplicity.

### Aims

1. The aim of L'Arche is to create communities which welcome people with a mental handicap. By this means, L'Arche seeks to respond to the distress of those who are too often rejected, and to give them a valid place in society.

2. L'Arche seeks to reveal the particular gifts of people with a mental handicap who belong at the very heart of their communities and who call others to share their lives.

3. L'Arche knows that it cannot welcome everyone who has a mental handicap. It seeks to offer not a solution but a sign, a sign that a society, to be truly human, must be founded on welcome and respect for the weak and the downtrodden.

4. In a divided world, L'Arche wants to be a sign of hope. Its communities, founded on covenant relationships between people of differing

117

intellectual capacity, social origin, religion and culture, seek to be signs of unity, faithfulness and reconciliation.

## Fundamental principles

1.  Whatever their gifts or their limitations, people are all bound together in a common humanity.

    Everyone is of unique and sacred value, and everyone has the same dignity and the same rights. The fundamental rights of each person include the right to life, to care, to a home, to education and to work.

    Also, since the deepest need of a human being is to love and to be loved, each person has a right to friendship, to communion and to a spiritual life.

2.  If human beings are to develop their abilities and talents to the full, realizing all their potential as individuals, they need an environment that fosters personal growth. They need to form relationships with others within families and communities. They need to live in an atmosphere of trust, security and mutual affection. They need to be valued, accepted and supported in real and warm relationships.

3.  People with a mental handicap often possess qualities of welcome, wonderment, spontaneity and directness. They are able to touch hearts and to call others to unity through their simplicity and vulnerability. In this way they are a living reminder to the wider world of the essential values of the heart without which knowledge, power and action lose their meaning and purpose.

4.  Weakness and vulnerability in a person, far from being an obstacle to union with God, can foster it. It is often through weakness, recognized and accepted, that the liberating love of God is revealed.

5.  In order to develop the inner freedom to which all people are called, and to grow in union with God, each person needs to have the opportunity of being rooted and nourished in a religious tradition.

## The communities

### 1.  Communities of Faith

1.1  L'Arche communities are communities of faith, rooted in prayer and trust in God. They seek to be guided by God and by their weakest members, through whom God's presence is revealed. Each community member is encouraged to discover and deepen his or her spiritual life and live it according to his or her particular faith and tradition. Those who have no religious affiliation are also welcomed and respected in their freedom of conscience.

1.2 Communities are either of one faith or inter-religious. Those which are Christian are either of one church or inter-denominational. Each community maintains links with the appropriate religious authorities and its members are integrated with local churches and other places of worship.

1.3 Communities recognize that they have an ecumenical vocation and a mission to work for unity.

## 2. Called to unity

2.1 Unity is founded on the covenant of love to which God calls all the community members. This implies welcome and respect for differences. Such unity presupposes that the person with a handicap is at the centre of community life.

This unity is built up over time and through faithfulness. Communities commit themselves to accompany their members (once their membership is confirmed) throughout their lives, if this is what those members want.

2.2 Home life is at the heart of a L'Arche community. The different members of a community are called to be one body. They live, work, pray and celebrate together, sharing their joys and their suffering and forgiving each other, as in a family. They have a simple life-style which gives priority to relationships.

2.3 The same sense of communion unites the various communities throughout the world. Bound together by solidarity and mutual commitment, they form a worldwide family.

## 3. Called to growth

3.1 L'Arche communities are places of hope. Each person, according to his or her own vocation, is encouraged to grow in love, self-giving and wholeness, as well as in independence, competence and the ability to make choices.

3.2 The communities wish to secure for their members education, work and therapeutic activities which will be a source of dignity, growth and fulfillment for them.

3.3 The communities wish to provide their members with the means to develop their spiritual life and to deepen their union with and love of God and other people.

3.4 All community members are invited to participate, as far as possible, in decisions concerning them.

## 4. *Integrated in society*

4.1 L'Arche communities are open and welcoming to the world around them. They form an integral part of life in their localities and seek to foster relationships with neighbours and friends.

4.2 The communities seek to be competent in all the tasks they are called to accomplish.

4.3 The communities wish to enable people with a handicap to work, believing work to be an important means of integration.

4.4 The communities seek to work closely with:

- ❑ the families and guardians of people who are handicapped
- ❑ professionals
- ❑ government authorities and with all those who work in a spirit of justice and peace for people who are handicapped.

## Conclusion

L'Arche is deeply concerned by the distress of people who suffer injustice and rejection because they are handicapped. This concern should impel the communities of L'Arche to do all they can to defend the rights of people with a mental handicap, to support the creation of places of welcome for them and to call our society to become more just and respectful towards them.

The communities of L'Arche want to be in solidarity with the poor of the world, and with all those who take part in the struggle for justice.

This Charter has been approved by the General Assembly of the Federation

Cap Rouge, May 1993

# APPENDIX 2

## L'Arche communities: Country
## and date of foundation

### FRANCE

| Name | Place | Date of foundation |
|---|---|---|
| L'Arche | Trosly-Breuil (Oise) | 1964 |
| La Merci | Courbillac (Charente) | 1969 |
| Les Trois Fontaines | Ambleteuse (Pas-de-Calais) | 1971 |
| L'Arc-en-Ciel | Paris | 1972 |
| La Rose des Vents | Verpillères (Somme) | 1975 |
| Moïta | Hauterives (Drôme) | 1976 |
| Le Moulin de l'Auro | L'Isle s/ la-Sorgue (Vaucluse) | 1977 |
| La Rebellerie | Nueil s/ Layon (Maine-et-Loire) | 1980 |
| Aigrefoin | St-Rémy-les-Chevreuse (Yvelines) | 1981 |
| Le Levain | Compiègne (Oise) | 1982 |
| L'Atre | Wambrechies (Nord) | 1983 |
| Le Sénevé | Nantes (Loir-Atlantique) | 1985 |
| Ecorchebeuf | Dieppe (Seine-Maritime) | 1985 |
| Le Caillou Blanc | Clohars-Fouesnant (Finistère) | 1987 |
| Les Sapins | Lignières-Sonneville (Charente) | 1987 |
| L'Olivier | Rennes (Ille-et-Vilaine) | 1989 |
| La Ruisselée | Saint-Mars d'Outillé (Sarthe) | 1989 |
| La Vigne | Dijon (Côte d'Or) | 1989 |
| La Croisée | Lyon (Rhône) | 1990 |

### CANADA

| Name | Place | Date of foundation |
|---|---|---|
| Daybreak | Toronto (Ontario) | 1969 |
| Alleluia House | Ottawa (Ontario) | 1972 |
| Shalom | Edmonton (Alberta) | 1972 |
| L'Arche Stratford | Stratford (Ontario) | 1973 |

| L'Arche Calgary | Calgary (Alberta) | 1973 |
|---|---|---|
| L'Arche Winnipeg | Winnipeg (Manitoba) | 1973 |
| L'Étable | Victoria (British Columbia) | 1973 |
| Shiloah | Vancouver (British Columbia) | 1974 |
| Le Printemps | Saint Malachie (Québec) | 1974 |
| L'Arche Arnprior | Arnprior (Ontario) | 1975 |
| L'Arche La Caravane | Green Valley (Ontario) | 1977 |
| L'Arche Agapé | Hull (Québec) | 1977 |
| L'Arche Hamilton | Hamilton (Ontario) | 1979 |
| L'Arche North Bay | North Bay (Ontario) | 1979 |
| L'Arche Montréal | Montréal (Québec) | 1979 |
| Homefires | Wolfeville (Nova Scotia) | 1983 |
| L'Arche Antigonish | Antigonish (Nova Scotia) | 1983 |
| L'Étoile | Québec (Québec) | 1983 |
| L'Arche Sudbury | Sudbury (Ontario) | 1983 |
| L'Arche Cape Breton | Why Cocomagh (Nova Scotia) | 1983 |
| Fleurs de Soleil | Beloeil (Québec) | 1985 |
| Le Saule Fragile | Amos (Québec) | 1986 |
| L'Arche Mauricie | Cap de la Madeleine (Québec) | 1987 |
| L'Arche Chinook | Lethbridge (Alberta) | 1992 |

## INDIA

| Asha Niketan | Bangalore | 1970 |
|---|---|---|
| Asha Niketan | Calcutta | 1972 |
| Asha Niketan | Kottivakkam (Madras) | 1975 |
| Asha Niketan | Nandi Bazaar (Kerala) | 1977 |

## DENMARK

| Niels Steensens Hus | Hensingor | 1972 |
|---|---|---|

## BELGIUM

| L'Arche Bruxelles | Brussels | 1973 |
|---|---|---|
| De Ark Antwerpen | Anvers | 1974 |
| Le Murmure | Aywaile (Liège) | 1976 |
| L'Arche Namur | Namur | 1977 |
| Aquero | Bierges | 1980 |

## UNITED STATES

| The Hearth | Erie (Pennsylvania) | 1973 |
|---|---|---|
| The Arch | Clinton (Iowa) | 1974 |
| Hope | Mobile (Alabama) | 1974 |
| L'Arche Syracuse | Syracuse (New York) | 1977 |

| L'Arche Cleveland | Cleveland (Ohio) | 1977 |
| Noah Sealth | Seattle (Washington) | 1981 |
| Tahoma Hope | Tacoma (Washington) | 1983 |
| Community of the Ark | Washington (D.C.) | 1984 |
| Irenicon | Bradford (Massachussets) | 1985 |
| L'Arche Spokane | Spokane (Washington) | 1986 |
| L'Arche Heartland | Kansas City (Kansas) | 1987 |
| L'Arche Nehalem | Portland (Oregon) | 1990 |
| Harbour House | Jacksonville (Floride) | 1992 |

## UNITED KINGDOM

| L'Arche Kent | Barfrestone (Kent) | 1974 |
| L'Arche Inverness | Inverness (Scotland) | 1975 |
| L'Arche Liverpool | Liverpool (England) | 1976 |
| L'Arche Lambeth | London | 1977 |
| L'Arche Bognor Regis | Bognor Regis | 1978 |
| L'Arche Brecon | Brecon (Wales) | 1989 |
| L'Arche Edinburgh | Edinburgh (Scotland) | 1992 |

## IVORY COAST

| L'Arche Bouaké | Bouaké | 1974 |

## HAÏTI

| L'Arche de Carrefour | Port-au-Prince | 1975 |
| L'Arche Chantal | Chantal (Cayes) | 1980 |

## HONDURAS

| El Arca de Honduras | Tegucigalpa | 1977 |
| Communidad del Arca | Choluteca | 1977 |

## AUSTRALIA

| Genesaret | Woden (Canberra) | 1978 |
| L'Arche Sydney | Burwood (Sydney) | 1983 |
| Beni Abbès | Hobart (Tasmania) | 1986 |

## BURKINA FASO

| Nongr Maasem | Ouagadougou | 1978 |

## IRELAND

| L'Arche Kilkenny | Kilkenny | 1978 |
| L'Arche Cork | Cork | 1984 |
| L'Arche Dublin | Dublin | 1993 |

## SPAIN

| | | |
|---|---|---|
| El Rusc | Tordera (Catalogne) | 1981 |
| El Avets | Moia (Catalogne) | 1989 |

## POLAND

| | | |
|---|---|---|
| Arka | Sledziejowice (Krakow) | 1981 |
| Arka | Poznam | 1994 |

## ITALY

| | | |
|---|---|---|
| Il Chicco | Ciampino (Rome) | 1983 |

## SWITZERLAND

| | | |
|---|---|---|
| la Corolle | Versoix (Geneva) | 1983 |
| Im Nauen | Hochwald (Bâle) | 1989 |
| La Grotte | Fribourg | 1993 |

## DOMINICAN REPUBLIC

| | | |
|---|---|---|
| El Arca de Santo Domingo | Santo Domingo | 1985 |

## MEXICO

| | | |
|---|---|---|
| El Arca de Mexico | Mexico | 1986 |

## BRAZIL

| | | |
|---|---|---|
| La Rocha | Sao Paolo | 1987 |

## GERMANY

| | | |
|---|---|---|
| Arche Regenbogen | Tecklenburg | 1987 |
| Arche Volksdorf | Hamburg | 1988 |

## PHILIPPINES

| | | |
|---|---|---|
| Punla | Manilla | 1988 |

## HUNGARY

| | | |
|---|---|---|
| Barka | Budapest | 1992 |

## JAPAN

| | | |
|---|---|---|
| Kana-no-ie | Shizuoka | 1992 |

## UGANDA

| | | |
|---|---|---|
| Arche Ouganda | Kampala | 1992 |

**Future topics in the**

# L'ARCHE COLLECTION

Personal and spiritual growth – Sue Mosteller

Service: The foot washing – Jean Vanier

L'Arche and the Third World – Robert Larouche

Accompaniment: Journeying together – Claire de Miribel

Ecumenism – Thérèse Vanier

Growth in Spirituality for Assistants and People with Handicaps – Eileen Glass